THE MILLION DOLLAR MOTHER

HOW MOMS BUILD EMPIRES WITHOUT BURNING OUT

AMULYA MISHRA

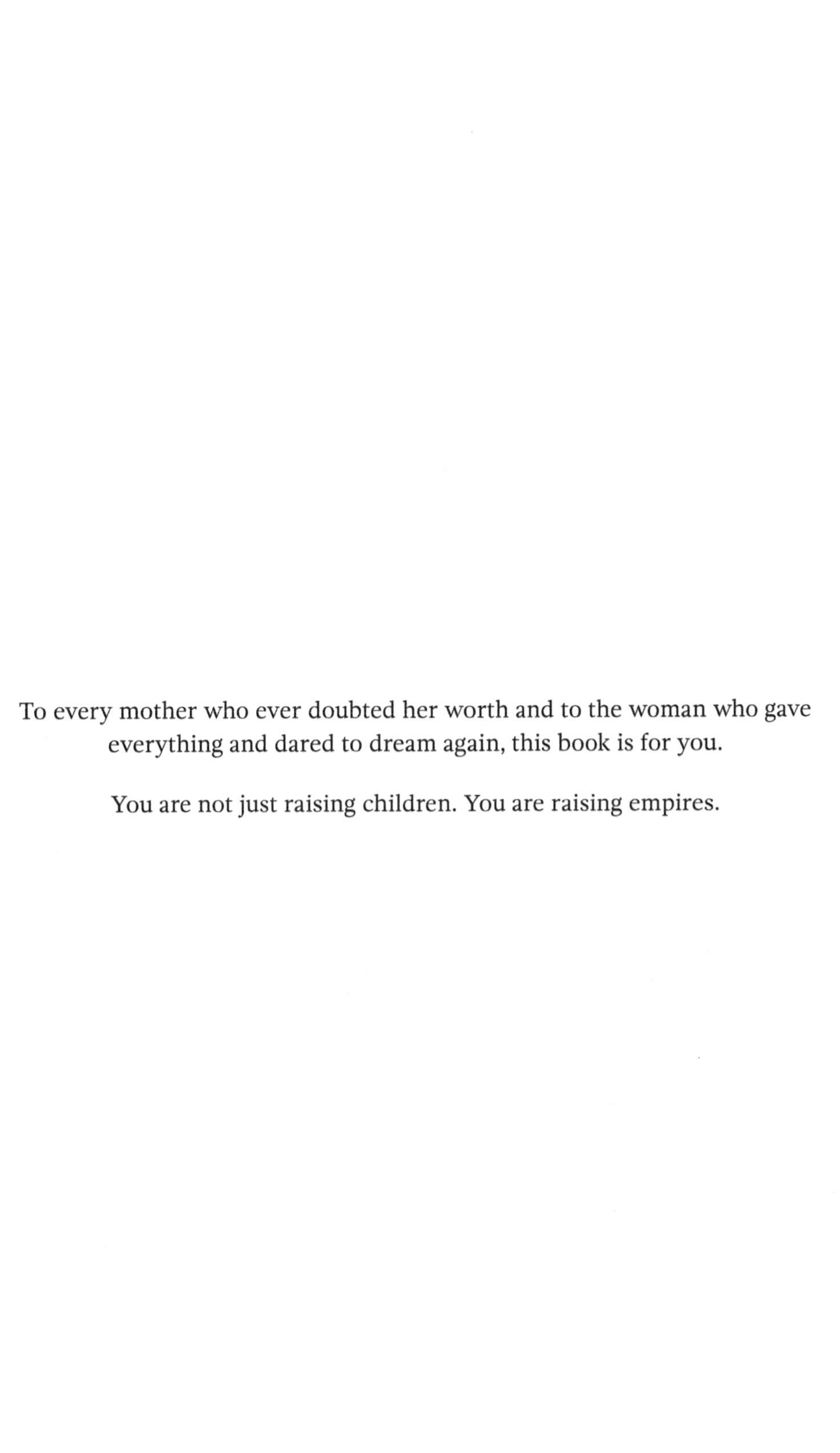

To every mother who ever doubted her worth and to the woman who gave everything and dared to dream again, this book is for you.

You are not just raising children. You are raising empires.

Contents

Contents

Contents

The Million Dollar Mother

How Moms Build Empires Without Burning Out

By Amulya Mishra

? She's not just raising a family. She's building a legacy.

? Power. Purpose. Profit—on her own terms.

Foreword

The world often underestimates the quiet power of a mother. Behind every packed lunch, every sleepless night, and every tear wiped away, there lies a force capable of shaking industries, transforming legacies, and redefining success on her own terms.

The Million Dollar Mother is more than just a book—it is a revolution. It dares to challenge the age-old myth that motherhood and ambition must live in separate worlds. It reminds us that the very traits that make a woman a nurturing parent—resilience, intuition, patience, emotional intelligence—are the same traits that make her a formidable entrepreneur, leader, and visionary.

Amulya Mishra has written a heartfelt, actionable, and deeply empowering guide that doesn't just speak to mothers—it elevates them. Page after page, he weaves wisdom with warmth, strategy with soul. Whether you're a new mom staring at a dream between diaper changes, or a seasoned mother rekindling a long-lost purpose, this book is your roadmap.

As you hold this book in your hands, know this: you are holding a permission slip. Permission to lead. To create. To rise—not in spite of your motherhood, but because of it.

This isn't about balance. It's about boldness. It's about building empires with grace and grit. And it begins here—with you

Preface

I didn't write this book because I had all the answers.

I wrote it because I had all the questions that every mother with a dream silently carries in her heart.

Can I be present for my children and still pursue my passion?

Can I build something meaningful without burning out?

Can I be a mother and still be me?

As a banker, an author, and someone raised by a woman who juggled a hundred invisible tasks without applause, I've seen firsthand how motherhood is often misread. Society sees soft hands and warm hugs. What it misses is the strategy behind every school drop, the resilience behind every sleepless night, and the quiet brilliance of a woman who leads her home like a CEO without ever being called one.

This book is my tribute to that woman.

It is not a manual for perfection. It is a manifesto for possibility.

Within these pages, you'll find stories, tools, and strategies not just to survive motherhood—but to thrive as a mother, creator, and visionary. You'll meet the version of yourself that isn't waiting for permission anymore—the one who's building wealth, wellness, and a legacy with fierce intention.

You are not behind. You are not alone. You are not limited.

You are a Million Dollar Mother.

Let this book remind you of that truth every time you doubt it.

With purpose and power,

Amulya Mishra

Acknowledgements

To write this book was to walk through the heart of every mother who has ever paused her dreams, whispered affirmations in the chaos, and risen quietly while the world was still asleep. This book would not exist without the countless women—seen and unseen—who continue to build empires with one hand while rocking the future with the other.

First, to my mother—you were my first example of strength disguised as softness. Your sacrifices, unspoken courage, and unwavering faith in possibility are etched into every word of this book.

To the mothers who messaged, mentored, and motivated me—your stories shaped this mission. Your resilience fueled each chapter. Thank you for showing me that motherhood is not a limitation; it is the launchpad.

To the readers—especially the women who have doubted themselves, questioned their worth, or shelved their ambitions—this book is for you. You are the reason this message matters. May every page remind you of the power you already possess.

To my family, who gave me space to write, and to my friends, who reminded me to breathe—thank you for your patience and belief.

Lastly, to every Million Dollar Mother reading this: I see you. I honor you. I believe in your journey.

With deep gratitude,
Amulya Mishra

Prologue

The Quiet Rise of the Unstoppable Mother

Before there was a title, before there was a brand, before there were strategies and affirmations—there was a woman.

She stood at the kitchen sink, half-dreaming between dishes. She scribbled ideas in the margins of school notebooks and whispered her ambitions into the silence of sleeping children. She wasn't loud. She wasn't famous. But she was powerful in ways the world had yet to name.

This book began with her.

With the mother who built her dreams between diaper changes and deadlines.

With the woman who carried both a child on her hip and a vision in her soul.

With the countless voices who asked, "Can I really do both?"—and dared to answer, "Yes."

The Million Dollar Mother isn't a fantasy. It's a future. One where mothers are not penalized for their softness but celebrated for their strength. One where wealth isn't measured only in numbers, but in peace, purpose, and legacy. One where motherhood is no longer the reason we stop—it's the reason we start.

You are not reading this by accident. You were called to these pages because something inside you is ready to rise. Ready to release the guilt. Ready to build with grace. Ready to remember that being a mother isn't the end of your identity—it's the awakening of your most powerful self.

Welcome to your next chapter.

It's not just business. It's not just motherhood.

It's becoming

TABLE OF CONTENTS

- Coaching & consulting from home

◆◆ Chapter 7: Passive Income Playbook—Small Starts, Big Gains
Main Focus: Smart investments and scalable income
◆◆

- Investing basics for mothers
- Saving and compounding strategies
- Royalties from digital products
- Side hustle automation
- Subscriptions and memberships

◆◆ Chapter 8: Raising Empowered Kids as You Build Your Empire
Main Focus: Combining parenting and leadership development
◆◆

- Teaching kids about money
- Involving children in your business
- Building emotional intelligence in kids
- Conscious parenting strategies
- Children as part of your legacy

◆◆ Chapter 9: Self-Care as a Million-Dollar Strategy
Main Focus: Why well-being is essential for success
◆◆

- Holistic wellness for mothers
- Ayurveda & yoga for energy reset
- Mental health maintenance
- Rituals for calm and clarity
- Burnout recovery and prevention

◆◆ Chapter 10: The Family Finance Formula
Main Focus: Personal and family wealth building
◆◆

- Budgeting with kids in mind

- Emergency fund building
- Insurance & protection for families
- Family goal-setting
- Teaching financial discipline to kids

◆◆ Chapter 11: Personal Branding for the Mom Next Door
Main Focus: Online presence for authority and income
◆◆

- Instagram and LinkedIn for moms
- Storytelling through motherhood
- Building trust with your audience
- Social media monetization
- Visual branding & niche marketing

◆◆ Chapter 12: Legacy: Leaving More Than Just Money
Main Focus: Creating generational impact
◆◆

- Writing a family mission statement
- Legacy journaling
- Storytelling as emotional inheritance
- Building a values-based estate
- Spiritual legacy and life lessons

Chapter 13: The Morning Power Hour—Starting Your Day Like a Millionaire Mom
Main Focus: Morning routines that energise and empower
Designing your Power Hour (mindset, movement, planning)

- Habit stacking for consistency
- Gratitude journaling & visualization
- Morning meditations & affirmations
- Energy-boosting habits (hydration, light, breathwork)

Chapter 14: Mom Boss Mindset—Rewiring Confidence Daily
Main Focus: Cultivating deep self-belief and resilience

Being a mompreneur takes more than skills—it takes unshakable belief. Confidence isn't something you're born with; it's something you practice. This chapter focuses on tools to boost your inner power.

- Power posing & body language
- Confidence journaling
- Affirmation scripting
- Visualization for fearless action
- Confidence-building micro wins

Chapter 15: Time to Hire Help—Outsourcing Without Guilt
Main Focus: Delegation for Freedom and Focus
Supermoms burn out trying to do it all. This chapter gives you permission to ask for and hire help at home and in your business.

- How to outsource affordably
- Delegating home tasks (cleaning, meal prep, childcare)
- Hiring VAs, editors, and designers
- Overcoming guilt and control
- Focusing on your zone of genius

Chapter 16: Creating Your Vision Map—Goal Setting with Heart & Hustle
Main Focus: Turning dreams into tangible, actionable plans
Goals without direction fade. Vision with structure grows. Learn how to map your goals with soul and strategy.

- Creating a vision board
- SMART goals + intuitive goals
- Quarterly goal mapping
- Weekly reflections and reviews
- Accountability systems for busy moms

Chapter 17: The Power of Saying No—Protecting Your Energy
Main Focus: Setting boundaries to honour your well-being
Every yes you give is a no to something else. This chapter empowers you to say "no" with love and clarity.

- Boundaries in business and parenting
- Scripted ways to decline politely
- Releasing people-pleasing tendencies
- Identifying your energy drains
- Building a YES list aligned with your goals

Chapter 18: Mompreneur Marketing 101—Visibility Without Burnout

Main Focus: Simple, authentic strategies to grow your brand

Marketing doesn't have to be overwhelming. This chapter offers mom-friendly systems to stay visible and sell with soul.

- Content batching & scheduling tools
- Repurposing one idea into many formats
- Personal storytelling in brand voice
- Free vs. paid promotions
- Building a content calendar

Chapter 19: Money Talks with Your Partner—Financial Alignment in Marriage

Main Focus: Growing together financially as a couple

Money can connect or divide. Learn how to have honest, empowering money conversations at home.

- Shared vs. separate accounts
- Monthly financial check-ins
- Setting money goals as a team
- Financial intimacy & conflict resolution
- Celebrating wins together

Chapter 20: Detox Your Digital Life—Reclaiming Focus in a Noisy World

Main Focus: Managing screen time for clarity and peace

Too much tech leads to distraction and anxiety. This chapter teaches you to build mindful tech habits that empower rather than exhaust.

- Phone-free mornings & nights
- Screen limits for moms and kids

- Unsubscribing & decluttering inboxes
- Focus apps and website blockers
- Creating a digital-free zone at home

Chapter 21: How to Handle Haters—Staying Grounded in a Loud World

Main Focus: Resilience in the face of criticism and online noise

Success comes with visibility—and visibility comes with critics. Learn to protect your peace and power.

- Understanding the psychology of trolls
- Strengthening your inner voice
- Strategies for handling negativity online
- When to respond and when to block
- Anchoring back to your purpose

Chapter 22: Celebrate Yourself—Anchoring Confidence Through Milestones

Main Focus: Building momentum through self-recognition

Too often, moms move from one task to the next without acknowledging their wins. Celebration is not just joy—it's fuel. It reinforces your identity as a capable, worthy woman. This chapter helps you create meaningful rituals to honor your growth.

- The psychology of positive reinforcement
- Weekly, monthly, and milestone celebrations
- Creating personal reward systems
- Journaling progress and micro wins
- Sharing success without shame

Chapter 23: The Entrepreneurial Motherhood Map—Balancing Growth and Grace

Main Focus: Navigating entrepreneurship with harmony, not hustle

This chapter explores how to scale your mission without sacrificing your motherhood.

- Planning around your family rhythm
- Business growth phases simplified

- Hiring help strategically
- Managing expectations with compassion
- The motherhood-business cycle: when to build, pause, and bloom

Chapter 24: The Power of Female Friendships—Sisterhood and Support

Main Focus: Building a circle that uplifts and energizes

A million-dollar mom doesn't rise alone. This chapter is about nurturing powerful relationships with other women.

- Identifying your circle of influence
- Navigating jealousy and comparison
- Mastermind groups and accountability partners
- Saying goodbye to draining friendships
- Hosting empowering circles at home or online

Chapter 25: Parenting While Pursuing Purpose—Embracing the Dual Role

Main Focus: Integrating your ambitions with your parenting journey

You're not choosing between being a great mom and a great visionary. You're becoming both—powerfully.

- Mompreneur guilt detox
- Aligning your values with how you parent and work
- Letting kids see the "real" you
- Creating structure that supports both roles
- When to ask for grace and when to go all in

Chapter 26: Selling With Soul—Authentic Marketing That Converts

Main Focus: Offering your gifts with confidence and clarity

Selling is a service. This chapter teaches soulful, mom-friendly sales strategies.

- Overcoming fear of selling
- Creating magnetic offers
- Conversational selling vs. pushy tactics
- Sales scripts with heart
- Follow up with love, not pressure.

Chapter 25: Parenting While Pursuing Purpose—Embracing the Dual Role

Main Focus: Integrating your ambitions with your parenting journey
Core Message: You're not choosing between being a great mom and a great visionary. You're becoming both—powerfully.

❖ 1: Mompreneur Guilt Detox

❖ 2: Aligning Your Values with How You Parent and Work

❖ 3: Letting Kids See the "Real" You

❖ 4: Creating Structure That Supports Both Roles

❖ 5: When to Ask for Grace and When to Go All In

Chapter 27: From Hustle to Harmony—Redefining Success on Your Terms

Main Focus: Letting go of "doing more" and choosing "being aligned"
The goal is not to do everything—it's to do what matters most. This chapter helps you build a success model based on your soul.

- Letting go of hustle culture
- Building a slow business with deep impact
- Rest as a business strategy
- Creating space to receive
- Inner alignment for outer results

Chapter 28: Healing the Inner Child—Becoming the Woman You Needed

Main Focus: Emotional healing and self-acceptance
Every mother carries an inner child. This chapter guides you through deep self-reflection and healing to unlock your full power.

- Identifying childhood wounds that block growth
- Reparenting rituals and forgiveness
- Visualization for healing
- Journaling conversations with your younger self
- Turning pain into purpose

Chapter 29: Creating a Home That Supports Your Dreams
Main Focus: Designing your environment for peace and productivity

Your home should inspire, not exhaust you. This chapter teaches space alignment for emotional and creative flow.

- Decluttering for clarity
- Designating a creative corner
- Feng Shui and energy flow basics
- Minimizing chaos in family zones
- Making home feel like your sanctuary

Chapter 30: Becoming Her—Embodying the Future You Now
Main Focus: Stepping into the identity of your higher self
It's not just about doing more—it's about becoming more. This chapter guides you to act, think, speak, and create like the woman you are becoming.

- Visualization practices
- Embodiment rituals
- Dressing, speaking, and choosing as your future self
- Emotional alignment with identity
- Manifestation meets micro action.

Your journey doesn't end at a milestone. It transforms. These final chapters are your invitation to live the million-dollar mindset—not someday, but every single day.

Chapter 1: Why Motherhood Is Your Superpower

Main Focus: Leverage maternal skills as entrepreneurial strengths.

Society often tells women that once they become mothers, their ambitions must shrink. But motherhood doesn't dim your light—it sharpens it. From early morning routines to late-night problem-solving, motherhood trains you in resilience, creativity, and leadership. This chapter flips the narrative, showing how motherhood isn't a setback but a secret weapon.

You've negotiated with toddlers. You've mastered multitasking. You've led a household. These aren't just chores—they're leadership traits. We'll explore how your everyday motherhood experiences actually cultivate skills that Fortune 500 CEOs spend years trying to learn.

You are already a decision-maker, a problem-solver, and a visionary. You've lived through exhaustion and still shown up with love. You've held space for others when you had none left for yourself. And now, it's time to channel that quiet power into purposeful growth.

Leadership Lessons from Motherhood

Mothers lead every single day—from managing routines to making crucial decisions about health, education, and home management. Whether it's organizing a child's school schedule, mediating sibling disputes, or running a household on a budget, mothers are constantly exercising leadership in real-time.

These leadership lessons translate seamlessly into the business world. The multitasking, critical thinking, and emotional control honed in motherhood are the very qualities that define successful entrepreneurs and CEOs. When a mother builds a routine that keeps a household running smoothly, she's practicing operational strategy. When she solves daily conflicts, she's developing conflict resolution skills that would make any HR professional proud.

If you can manage a toddler tantrum in a grocery store, you can lead a boardroom. If you can plan a week of nutritious meals on a tight budget, you can develop a lean business strategy. If you can organize a birthday party for twenty kids, you can definitely handle project management.

Mothers have what many corporations are desperately trying to teach their leaders: calm under pressure, empathy, accountability, vision, and stamina. These aren't theoretical ideas. They're lived experiences. Your motherhood has already made you a leader—now it's time to own that power and redirect it into your next venture, whether it's a business, a book, or a movement.

Affirmation: I am already a leader. Every decision I make as a mother strengthens my power to lead in business and life.

Emotional Intelligence and Resilience

Mo)therhood is the ultimate emotional boot camp. From the moment your child is born, you're navigating an emotional rollercoaster—your own and theirs. Whether it's calming a screaming toddler, comforting a heartbroken teen, or managing the ups and downs of your own identity shift, you are constantly tuning into emotional signals and responding with empathy, patience, and strength.

This is emotional intelligence in action.

In the business world, emotional intelligence is considered one of the top predictors of success. It helps in managing teams, resolving conflicts, building customer relationships, and creating healthy workplace environments. As a mother, you've already mastered many of these skills. You anticipate needs before they're spoken. You de-escalate tension with a soothing voice. You coach, encourage, and uplift. These are traits that money can't buy—but motherhood teaches for free.

Then there's resilience—the silent power that keeps mothers going when they're running on two hours of sleep, dealing with health scares, or facing financial stress. Resilience is not about never falling; it's about rising every time you do. Mothers rise every single day.

When your child is sick, you don't get to give up. When the world feels overwhelming, you don't check out. That mental toughness—paired with emotional depth—is what makes mothers some of the most adaptable and powerful leaders in the world.

In business, things go wrong. People disappoint. Plans fail. But with the emotional grounding and bounce-back ability you've already built as a mother, you're equipped to weather the storms and keep going. You don't just survive—you evolve.

Affirmation: My emotional intelligence is a superpower. My resilience is my edge. I was built for breakthroughs, not breakdowns.

Decision-Making Under Pressure (Daily Parenting as Training!)

If there's one skill mothers develop to an elite level, it's the ability to make rapid decisions under pressure. From deciding whether your child's cough needs a doctor's visit to preparing meals while managing a meltdown to handling school deadlines, emergencies, and emotional needs—all in one afternoon—your brain has been wired to analyze, act, and adapt in seconds.

This is the exact kind of decision-making that leaders, entrepreneurs, and executives are trained to develop. But you didn't need a fancy degree to get it. You've lived it—daily.

In business, every opportunity, challenge, and shift requires strong decision-making. Should you launch this product now or wait? Should you invest in that idea? How do you pivot when something fails? The pressure is real—but so are your instincts, sharpened by motherhood. You've had to make difficult choices, and fast ones, without always having perfect information—just like in entrepreneurship.

The truth is, most corporate professionals are taught to "analyze before they act." Mothers learn to "act while analyzing." That difference is a competitive edge. Your gut instinct, honed through years of micro-decisions and crisis handling, is your boardroom compass.

Motherhood gives you clarity. You learn to separate what matters from the noise. You've learned to act decisively when it counts. Now, it's time to trust that instinct in your business, your career, and your future.

Affirmation: I trust my instincts. I am capable of making powerful decisions under pressure because I've been doing it every single day.

Communication Skills from Parenting

Mothers are expert communicators. Whether you're explaining bedtime routines to toddlers, negotiating with a stubborn teen, or calming an anxious child, you are constantly tailoring your tone, message, and delivery to your audience.

This is a goldmine of experience when it comes to running a business or building a brand. You know how to read between the lines. You can sense emotions beneath words. You've become a pro at simplifying complex topics, making people feel heard, and resolving conflicts with compassion.

These communication skills are essential for:

- Customer service
- Team management
- Marketing and sales
- Public speaking
- Writing persuasive content

Apply your parenting communication framework to your professional life: empathize, simplify, redirect, and empower.

Affirmation: My voice is powerful. I communicate with clarity, connection, and care.

Real-Life Examples of Successful Mompreneurs

To bring it all home, look at the women who've walked this path:

- **Jessica Alba** turned her frustration with unsafe baby products into The Honest Company, now worth over a billion dollars.
- **Sara Blakely** launched Spanx while working full-time and became the youngest self-made female billionaire.
- **Julie Aigner-Clark** created Baby Einstein with home videos—later bought by Disney.
- **Ashleigh Evans**, mom of two, built her cocktail kit brand InBooze during the pandemic and scaled it through Instagram.
- **Kavita Nair**, founder of BabyBerry in India, created a parenting health tech platform to support other mothers.

These stories prove one thing: motherhood doesn't limit your success—it fuels it.

Affirmation: If they can, I can. I am not alone on this path. My journey as a mother is my business advantage—not my obstacle.

Final Reflection:

Motherhood isn't a pause. It's a launchpad. You've already built systems, nurtured humans, and managed chaos with grace. Now, it's time to take those skills and build your dream. Because the world doesn't just need more entrepreneurs—it needs more empowered mothers leading the way.

Chapter 2: The Mindset Shift—From Guilt to Greatness

Main Focus: Dismantling guilt and cultivating a winner's mindset

The greatest block to a mother's success is not a lack of time, resources, or talent—it's guilt. Silent. Heavy. Unrelenting. Guilt that whispers, "You're not doing enough," even when you're giving your all. Guilt that says success must come at the cost of your family. But what if we told you that greatness and motherhood not only coexist but also amplify each other?

This chapter is your permission slip to drop the guilt and pick up your crown. The journey from guilt to greatness starts with one shift: believing you are worthy of both success and softness. Of leadership and love. Of impact and presence.

❖ ❖ Overcoming "Mom Guilt"

Problem: Society has glamorized martyrdom in motherhood, celebrating the mother who gives up everything while forgetting herself.

Insight: Psychologists confirm that guilt, when internalized long-term, leads to stress, poor self-image, and burnout. Guilt is useful only when it alerts us to a misstep—not when it becomes our identity.

Solution: Redefine what being a good mother means. It's not about perfection—it's about presence, love, and alignment. A fulfilled mom is a powerful one. Choosing your dreams isn't abandoning your kids—it's inspiring them.

Practical Exercise: Write down three things you feel guilty about. For each, reframe it as a conscious, empowered choice. Replace guilt with gratitude.

Affirmation: I am enough. I release guilt and choose joy—for myself and my children.

❖ ❖ 2: Reprogramming Limiting Beliefs

Problem: We inherit beliefs like "I can't have it all," "Mothers aren't meant to be wealthy," or "Now isn't the time." These beliefs aren't facts—they're conditioning.

Insight: Neuroscience proves that repeated thoughts form pathways in the brain. But those pathways can be rewritten through repetition, visualization, and action.

Solution: Identify 3–5 limiting beliefs holding you back. For each, write a counter-belief that feels empowering. Then speak it aloud daily.

Practical Tools:

* Mirror work (look into your eyes and declare your truth)
* Write "I believe" statements.
* Record empowering audios in your voice.

Affirmation: My past does not define my future. I am rewriting my story every day.

❖❖ Developing a Wealth Mindset

Problem: Many moms feel guilt around money—feeling greedy for wanting more or fearful they aren't "smart enough" to handle it.

Insight: Wealth is a tool—not a measure of your worth. When women have wealth, families thrive, communities grow, and generations are lifted.

Solution: Practice abundance thinking. Celebrate money as energy—meant to flow, serve, and multiply. Start small: track income, celebrate every sale, and speak about money goals without shame.

Mindset Shift: From "I can't afford this" to "How can I create the income for this?"

Practical Step: Set a weekly money date—review your finances, set goals, and express gratitude for every rupee/dollar received.

Affirmation: I deserve wealth. I attract abundance with every empowered choice I make.

❖❖ Positive Self-Talk and Affirmations for Mothers

Problem: The inner voice of a mother can often be her harshest critic.

Insight: According to CBT (Cognitive Behavioral Therapy), thoughts shape behavior. Self-talk affects self-worth, energy, and confidence.

Solution: Replace "I'm failing" with "I'm learning." Replace "I'm behind" with "I'm exactly where I need to be."

Daily Affirmation Ritual:

* Morning: 3 affirmations before checking your phone
* Midday: Breath + one empowering phrase

- Night: One gratitude-focused statement

Affirmation: I speak to myself with love. My words build worlds inside and out.

◆◆ 5: Neuroplasticity & Emotional Healing for Moms

Problem: Emotional exhaustion, trauma, or comparison can make growth feel impossible.

Insight: The brain is elastic. Through focused thought, habit changes, and emotional tools, you can reshape your experience at any age.

Solution: Combine practices like

- Journaling
- Meditation
- Visualization
- EFT (Emotional Freedom Technique or "tapping")
- Gratitude rewiring

30-Day Brain Rewire Challenge:

- 5 minutes of gratitude writing
- 2 minutes of breathwork
- 1 empowering visualization

Affirmation: I am healing. I am growing. My mind is my garden, and I choose to plant peace.

Expanded Final Reflection:

Guilt is not your home. Doubt is not your destiny. You were never meant to stay small to make others comfortable. You were never meant to disappear behind sacrifice. Your greatness is not a future version of you—it's the woman reading this right now.

You can be a present, loving mother and a powerful, wealthy woman. You can take up space, set boundaries, speak big dreams, and still be the soft place your child runs to. Your family doesn't need your perfection—they need your truth.

The mindset shift begins when you choose yourself—not in spite of motherhood, but because of it.

Final Affirmation: I am guilt-free, greatness-bound, and exactly where I need to be to rise.

Chapter 3: Building Income Streams That Work While You Sleep Main Focus: Creating passive and semi-passive income

Imagine waking up to a message that says, "You just earned ₹500." That's the power of passive income. It doesn't mean zero effort—it means building systems and products that continue to earn even when you're not actively working. For moms, this isn't just ideal—it's essential. Your energy is precious, and your time is limited. This chapter empowers you to build income streams that support your lifestyle, your goals, and your family.

❖❖ 1: Investing Basics for Mothers

Problem: Many mothers feel investing is risky or confusing.

Insight: Starting small builds confidence. You don't need to be wealthy to invest—you just need consistency and a plan.

Solution:

- Open a SIP (Systematic Investment Plan).
- Learn about low-risk mutual funds.
- Use beginner-friendly apps like Zerodha, Groww, or INDmoney.

Practical Tip: Start with ₹100– ₹500 a week. Set up auto-debit. Let it grow.

Affirmation: I am an investor. Every rupee I earn today creates freedom tomorrow.

❖❖ 2: Saving and Compounding Strategies

Problem: Savings often get delayed due to daily family expenses.

Insight: Saving isn't about amount—it's about habit. Compounding makes small amounts grow significantly over time.

Solution:

- Use the 50-30-20 rule: 50% needs, 30% wants, and 20% savings.
- Open a high-interest savings account.
- Automate savings weekly.

Practical Tip: Label your savings accounts by goal. "Vacation," "Kids' Future," "Freedom Fund."

Affirmation: My money multiplies with ease. My savings create security and abundance.

◆◆ 3: Royalties from Digital Products

Problem: Trading time for money limits income potential.

Insight: Digital products let you create once and earn forever.

Solution:

- Write an eBook (Amazon KDP)
- Create a printable planner (Etsy, Gumroad).
- Record a mini-course or workshop.

Practical Tip: Focus on problems you've already solved. Start with one 10-page PDF or video series.

Affirmation: I earn while I sleep. My knowledge and creativity pay me back endlessly.

◆◆ 4: Side Hustle Automation

Problem: Managing clients, orders, and content gets overwhelming fast.

Insight: Automation tools reduce manual work and increase income without burnout.

Solution:

- Use ConvertKit or Mailchimp for email automation.
- Use Notion or Trello to organize business workflows.
- Schedule social media with Later or Buffer.

Practical Tip: Start with automating one thing—like welcome emails or content posting.

Affirmation: I work smart. My systems support me even when I rest.

◆◆ 5: Subscriptions and Memberships

Problem: One-time sales don't guarantee steady income.

Insight: Subscription models provide recurring revenue and community.

Solution:

- Start a monthly club: "Mindful Moms Circle" or "Millionaire Mom Book Club."

- Offer value: exclusive content, Q&As, resources
- Use Patreon, Podia, or a private WhatsApp group.

Practical Tip: Start small— ₹99/month with clear, consistent value.

Affirmation: My income is consistent. I serve with heart and receive with ease.

Final Reflection:

You don't need to trade hours for income forever. You don't need to hustle harder—you need to create smarter. Let your money work for you. Let your skills, stories, and systems

CHAPTER IV

Chapter 4: Mom Guilt vs. Mom Goals Main Focus: Balancing personal ambition with emotional well-being

Every ambitious mother has felt it—that tug of guilt when working on her dreams. The internal voice that says, "You're missing out" or "You should be doing more for your kids." But here's the truth: Guilt thrives in silence and disappears in clarity. This chapter is about turning guilt into grace, showing you that you can pursue your goals and be a deeply present mother. Not only are these two identities not in conflict—they strengthen each other.

�� 1: Emotional Freedom Techniques (EFT)

Problem: Emotional overwhelm creates guilt spirals, leading to procrastination or emotional burnout.

Insight: EFT, or tapping, is a powerful tool backed by psychology to reduce stress, anxiety, and guilt in minutes.

Solution:

- Learn the 7 tapping points: eyebrow, side of eye, under eye, under nose, chin, collarbone, and top of head.
- Create a daily script like, "Even though I feel guilty, I deeply and completely accept myself."

Practical Tip: Tap for 3 minutes every morning or before doing something for yourself.

Affirmation: I release guilt. I choose peace and progress.

�� 2: Setting Healthy Boundaries

Problem: Moms often say "yes" to everything, leaving little space for personal growth.

Insight: Boundaries aren't walls—they're doors that open to self-respect and alignment.

Solution:

- Use clear language: "That doesn't work for me." "I'm not available," or "I need time for this."
- Set boundaries with phone time, work hours, and emotional labor.

Practical Tip: Write your top 3 boundaries and place them visibly as reminders.

Affirmation: My boundaries are loving. They protect my time, energy, and vision.

❖❖ 3: Teaching Your Kids to Understand Your Goals

Problem: Moms fear that ambition makes their kids feel second place.

Insight: Children who see moms chase dreams grow up believing they can too.

Solution:

- Involve them in your work: Show your planner and explain what you're building.
- Celebrate goals together: when you hit a milestone, let them ring a bell or plan a mini party.

Practical Tip: Create a "family vision board" with each member's goals.

Affirmation: I lead with love. My goal is to teach my children what's possible.

❖❖ 4: Journaling and Emotional Detox

Problem: Suppressed guilt leads to emotional clutter and resentment.

Insight: Journaling helps you understand your emotions, reset intentions, and forgive yourself.

Solution:

- Use prompts like "What am I proud of today?" "What do I need to release?" "How did I show up for myself and my family?"

Practical Tip: Keep a journal by your bedside. Write for 5 minutes at night—release what doesn't serve you.

Affirmation: My emotions are valid. I express them freely and let them flow.

❖❖ 5: Reframing "Selfishness" into Self-Priority

Problem: Many moms mistake self-care for neglecting their family.

Insight: Prioritizing yourself is an act of leadership, not laziness.
Solution:

- Shift the narrative: "I'm not being selfish—I'm investing in my wholeness."
- Schedule one non-negotiable joy activity every week (reading, walking, dancing).

Practical Tip: Rename your calendar block from "me time" to "energy recharge."
Affirmation: Prioritizing myself isn't selfish—it's sacred.
Final Reflection:
Mom guilt is real—but so are your goals. You don't have to choose between being present and being powerful. Every time you choose growth, your children learn that they can too. You are not abandoning them—you're modeling boldness, courage, and self-love. Release the guilt, honor your goals, and remember: your light doesn't dim their shine—it helps them see the way.

Chapter 5: Digital Business Ideas for the Modern Mother Main Focus: Online business models that work for moms

The digital economy has opened doors like never before—especially for moms. With just a phone, Wi-Fi, and a dream, mothers around the world are turning their skills, stories, and time into thriving online businesses. Whether you have five hours or five minutes a day, there's a model that fits your life and your energy.

This chapter breaks down simple, scalable digital business ideas that give you freedom, income, and impact—all from home.

❖❖ 1: Digital Course Creation

Problem: Moms have valuable experience but don't know how to package it.

Insight: If you've solved a problem (toddler sleep training, budgeting, meal planning), others want your shortcut.

Solution:

- Use platforms like Teachable, Thinkific, or Canva + Gumroad to launch courses.
- Keep it simple: 3–5 video lessons, a worksheet, and a result

Practical Tip: Record lessons using your smartphone. Offer a free class to collect testimonials.

Affirmation: My knowledge is valuable. My course changes lives and creates income.

❖❖ 2: Virtual Assistant Business

Problem: Moms want flexible work but not full-time commitments.

Insight: Every online business needs support—social media, email, scheduling, and customer service.

Solution:

- Offer VA services on Fiverr, Upwork, or through referrals.

- Specialize in something simple (Pinterest VA, Canva design, email replies).

Practical Tip: Start by offering free work to one client for a testimonial. Build a simple portfolio on Canva.

Affirmation: I serve with skill. I work from home on my terms and build a steady income.

◆◆ 3: Selling on Amazon, Etsy, or Shopify

Problem: Moms love creating but feel overwhelmed by shipping and stock.

Insight: Print-on-demand and dropshipping eliminate inventory and allow creativity.

Solution:

- Use Printful or Teespring for mugs, shirts, and journals.
- Use Amazon KDP to publish blank journals, workbooks, or storybooks.
- Use Etsy for handmade crafts or digital downloads.

Practical Tip: Create one product this week (a gratitude journal or mom planner) and upload it.

Affirmation: I create once and earn often. My creativity supports my family and others.

◆◆ 4: Mom-Focused Content Creation (Reels, Blogs, eBooks)

Problem: Moms underestimate their voice and assume nobody wants to hear their story.

Insight: Real, relatable stories connect deeply. If you've felt something, so has someone else.

Solution:

- Share parenting wins and fails via Instagram Reels or YouTube Shorts.
- Write blogs on Medium or Substack.
- Self-publish eBooks on Kindle (how-to guides, stories, advice).

Practical Tip: Set a weekly schedule: 1 video, 1 blog, 1 short post. Repurpose everything.

Affirmation: My voice matters. My content creates community and cash flow.

� � 5: Coaching & Consulting from Home

Problem: Moms with professional or life expertise don't know how to monetize it.

Insight: Coaching is about guiding others through something you've already mastered.

Solution:

- Offer 1:1 coaching on Zoom (parenting, wellness, confidence, business).
- Use Calendly for scheduling and Zoom or WhatsApp for delivery.

Practical Tip: Offer 3 free discovery calls to get testimonials and refine your offer.

Affirmation: I coach with heart. My guidance transforms lives and supports my purpose.

Final Reflection:

The online world isn't just a marketplace—it's your canvas. You don't need permission. You need a platform. Start small. Show up messy. Let your growth inspire your kids. Because the modern mother doesn't just raise children—she raises impact, income, and influence.

Chapter 6: Passive Income Playbook—Small Starts, Big Gains Main Focus: Smart investments and scalable income

Passive income isn't about doing nothing. It's about doing the work once and letting your systems, products, or investments do the heavy lifting. As a mother, your time is sacred. Passive income allows you to multiply your impact without multiplying your hours. This chapter focuses on low-barrier, realistic options for moms ready to build wealth in their sleep.

❖❖ 1: Investing Basics for Mothers

Problem: Investing seems intimidating and risky for beginners.

Insight: Starting small with basic tools builds confidence. You don't need ₹10,000—you need ₹100 and consistency.

Solution:

- Begin with SIPs, index funds, or micro-investing apps like Groww, Zerodha, or INDmoney.
- Focus on long-term growth, not quick wins.

Practical Tip: Set up auto-debit for ₹100 per week into a mutual fund or SIP. Watch your wealth compound.

Affirmation: I am an investor. Every rupee I earn today builds freedom for tomorrow.

❖❖ 2: Saving and Compounding Strategies

Problem: With family needs, saving often takes a backseat.

Insight: Compounding turns small savings into long-term security. The earlier you start, the bigger the impact.

Solution:

- Use the 20% rule: Save at least 20% of every income.
- Label your savings with emotional goals: "Freedom Fund," "Dream Trip," "Kid's Future"

Practical Tip: Open separate savings accounts and automate small weekly transfers.

Affirmation: My savings grow steadily. I create peace, not pressure, with every choice.

❖❖ 3: Royalties from Digital Products

Problem: Trading time for money limits your freedom.

Insight: Digital products let you serve people while sleeping, parenting, or vacationing.

Solution:

- Create digital items like journals, templates, guides, or audio courses.
- Sell them on platforms like Gumroad, Payhip, Amazon KDP, Notion press Etsy.

Practical Tip: Start with one product: a 10-page PDF guide or a printable planner. Keep it simple; solve a problem.

Affirmation: I earn while I rest. My creativity continues to serve and sell.

❖❖ 4: Side Hustle Automation

Problem: You want income, but your hands are full.

Insight: Smart automation saves time and multiplies reach.

Solution:

- Automate customer emails (Convert Kit)
- Use Notion or Trello for workflow management.
- Schedule social content with Later or Meta Business Suite.

Practical Tip: Start with automating your client onboarding or newsletter welcome emails.

Affirmation: I work with ease. My systems work when I don't.

❖❖ 5: Subscriptions and Memberships

Problem: One-time sales can feel unpredictable.

Insight: Membership models bring monthly recurring revenue—and community.

Solution:

- Start a low-cost membership: ₹199/month for monthly mom circles, workshops, or digital drops.

- Deliver value consistently via WhatsApp, Telegram, or Patreon.

Practical Tip: Name your membership something inspiring like "Empowered Mom Network" or "Soulful Wealth Circle."

Affirmation: I create consistent income. My community thrives with my leadership.

Final Reflection:

Passive income doesn't mean passive intention. It means choosing leverage over hustle. A digital product. An investment plan. A monthly membership. These are your new tools of time and wealth freedom. Start small. Think big. You are not behind—you are building.

Chapter 7: Raising Empowered Kids as You Build Your Empire Main Focus: Combining parenting and leadership development

Being a mom doesn't mean putting your dreams on hold. It means building your empire with your children by your side. In fact, motherhood offers the perfect environment to raise not just great kids but future leaders. This chapter shows you how to empower your children while pursuing your goals, proving that your legacy starts with who you raise, not just what you build.

❖❖ 1: Teaching Kids About Money

Problem: Financial literacy is often overlooked in early parenting.

Insight: Kids absorb habits from what they see—not just what they're taught.

Solution:

- Use three jars or wallets labeled "Spend, Save, and Share.
- Let kids manage small allowances and make low-stakes decisions.

Practical Tip: Involve your children in small family purchases and explain how budgeting works.

Affirmation: I raise money-wise children. Their future is built on wisdom and intention.

❖❖ 2: Involving Children in Your Business

Problem: Moms often feel guilt for spending time on work.

Insight: Kids become more curious, confident, and creative when they see how businesses are built.

Solution:

- Let kids help with age-appropriate tasks like labeling, packing, and filming behind-the-scenes videos.
- Explain your goals and let them cheer you on when you reach milestones.

Practical Tip: Create a "CEO Hour" where your child co-works with you once a week.

Affirmation: My work is a legacy. My children learn by watching me build with love.

◆◆ 3: Building Emotional Intelligence in Kids

Problem: Kids today face more emotional overwhelm than ever before.

Insight: Emotionally intelligent children perform better in school, relationships, and leadership.

Solution:

- Daily check-ins with simple questions: "How are you feeling today?"
- Teach vocabulary for emotions and let them express themselves without fear.

Practical Tip: Start a "Feelings Journal" where your child can draw or write a daily emotion.

Affirmation: I nurture emotional strength. My children are seen, safe, and supported.

◆◆ 4: Conscious Parenting Strategies

Problem: Traditional discipline models can create fear rather than growth.

Insight: Conscious parenting focuses on empathy, presence, and modeling behavior over control.

Solution:

- Pause before reacting. Ask, "What do they need emotionally right now?"
- Focus on connection before correction.

Practical Tip: Use positive reinforcement more than punishment. Celebrate good behavior with affirmations.

Affirmation: I lead with love. I parent with presence, not pressure.

◆◆ 5: Children as Part of Your Legacy

Problem: Many moms focus so hard on providing that they forget to pass on vision.

Insight: True legacy isn't what you leave for your kids—it's what you leave in them.

Solution:

- Share your core values often. integrity, freedom, courage, joy
- Let your kids see your vision board or create one as a family.

Practical Tip: Write a "legacy letter" to your kids about who you are and what matters most to you.

Affirmation: My legacy lives in them. I raise leaders, not followers.

Final Reflection:

Your children don't need a perfect parent. They need a present, powerful one. Let them watch you rise. Let them hear you speak affirmations. Let them feel the courage it takes to dream big. Because every step you take toward your goals is a step you take on behalf of their future.

Chapter 8: Self-Care as a Million-Dollar Strategy Main Focus: Why well-being is essential for success

Your business can only grow as far as you are well. Burnout is not a badge of honor—it's a warning sign. In a world that glorifies hustle, self-care is your rebellion. As a mother and entrepreneur, your body is your engine, your mind is your compass, and your heart is your fuel. This chapter reframes self-care from luxury to necessity—your most strategic investment.

� � 1: Holistic Wellness for Mothers

Problem: Moms often neglect their health in the name of serving everyone else.

Insight: Wellness isn't just physical—it's emotional, spiritual, and energetic.

Solution:

- Build a wellness routine around hydration, movement, sleep, and joy.
- Focus on consistency over complexity.

Practical Tip: Create a "daily wellness check" with 4 questions: Did I move? Did I hydrate? Did I rest? Did I smile?

Affirmation: I nurture my whole self. Wellness is my baseline for greatness.

� � 2: Ayurveda & Yoga for Energy Reset

Problem: Mental fog and fatigue reduce focus and energy.

Insight: Ancient practices like yoga and Ayurveda help regulate mood, digestion, and emotional clarity.

Solution:

- Identify your dosha (Vata, Pitta, or Kapha).
- Use tailored practices: grounding foods, restorative yoga, and herbal teas.

Practical Tip: Start the day with lemon water, 10 minutes of yoga, and mindful breathing.

Affirmation: My body is intelligent. I honor it through stillness and flow.

❖❖ 3: Mental Health Maintenance

Problem: Emotional load and invisible stress lead to mental burnout.

Insight: Mental health is not a crisis tool—it's a daily discipline.

Solution:

- Block time weekly for emotional check-ins (journaling, therapy, coaching).
- Use the "3-S" model: silence, support, and storytelling.

Practical Tip: Replace scrolling with a 10-minute guided meditation before bed.

Affirmation: My mind is sacred. I protect it with peace and perspective.

❖❖ 4: Rituals for Calm and Clarity

Problem: Life moves fast. Peace must be created on purpose.

Insight: Rituals anchor your nervous system and create structure amidst chaos.

Solution:

- Morning ritual: water, breath, stretch, gratitude
- Evening ritual: journal, candlelight, herbal tea

Practical Tip: Create a "ritual corner" with a cushion, diffuser, journal, and soft music.

Affirmation: I am rooted in calm. My rituals refill me daily.

❖❖ 5: Burnout Recovery and Prevention

Problem: Constant giving without receiving leads to resentment, fatigue, and breakdowns.

Insight: Burnout is a signal—not a sentence. Recovery begins with permission.

Solution:

- Identify your burnout type: physical, emotional, or creative.
- Say "no" more often. Rest before you're depleted.

Practical Tip: Plan one "non-negotiable joy break" per week. Guilt-free.

Affirmation: I rest with intention. Recovery is my strategy for long-term power.

Final Reflection:

Self-care isn't selfish—it's your secret weapon. Your strength lives in your softness. Your clarity comes from your calm. When you prioritize yourself, you model self-worth to your family, your business, and your future. Wellness is wealth. Protect it like a queen.

Chapter 9: The Family Finance Formula Main Focus: Personal and family wealth building

Money is not just a tool—it's a language your family speaks every day. Whether in the form of stress, decisions, or dreams, financial conversations shape how your children view wealth and worth. This chapter gives you the blueprint to take control of your finances, align your family with shared goals, and model abundance for future generations.

◆◆ 1: Budgeting with Kids in Mind

Problem: Family budgeting often overlooks emotional goals and shared experiences.

Insight: A budget isn't about restriction—it's about reflection. It should reflect your values, dreams, and realities.

Solution:

- Use a three-category system: Musts (needs), Joys (wants), and Future (savings/investments).
- Involve your kids in budget planning for small things (vacations, family nights).

Practical Tip: Create a visual budget board for the whole family to see and contribute to.

Affirmation: Our money reflects our dreams. We budget with love and clarity.

◆◆ 2: Emergency Fund Building

Problem: One unexpected expense can derail emotional and financial security.

Insight: An emergency fund builds not just savings—but safety and confidence.

Solution:

- Start with a small goal (₹5,000–₹10,000) and build in tiers.
- Store it in a separate, easy-to-access savings account.

Practical Tip: Sell unused items or start a weekend hustle to jumpstart your emergency stash.

Affirmation: We are protected. Our peace is backed by preparation.

❖❖ 3: Insurance & Protection for Families

Problem: Many families delay insurance thinking they don't need it yet.

Insight: Insurance is a love letter to your future—it's care in advance.

Solution:

- Review life, health, and home insurance annually.
- Choose plans that match your life stage, not just your income.

Practical Tip: Keep a "Protection Folder" with all key policies, contacts, and instructions.

Affirmation: Our family is covered. Our future is safe and secure.

❖❖ 4: Family Goal-Setting

Problem: Most families don't sit together to create a vision.

Insight: Goals build unity. When kids feel included, they grow with pride and purpose.

Solution:

- Host quarterly family goal nights.
- Create shared short-, mid-, and long-term goals.

Practical Tip: Use colored sticky notes or whiteboards to track progress visually in your home.

Affirmation: We grow together. Our goals connect and uplift us.

❖❖ 5: Teaching Financial Discipline to Kids

Problem: Schools don't teach real-world money habits early enough.

Insight: Discipline isn't about denial—it's about direction.

Solution:

- Introduce concepts like interest, saving, and giving early through play and real-life practice.
- Use apps like PiggyVest or FamZoo for hands-on learning.

Practical Tip: Create a family finance hour once a month. Play games, share money goals, and celebrate wins.

Affirmation: My children are wise with money. They grow with respect, joy, and knowledge.

Final Reflection:

You don't need to be a finance expert to build wealth—you need intention, alignment, and action. When your family speaks the language of money with joy, unity, and purpose, you create generational security and empowerment. Start where you are. Lead with love. Build a legacy.

CHAPTER X

Chapter 10: Personal Branding for the Mom Next Door Main Focus: Online presence for authority and income

In the digital age, your name is your brand. It's not about perfection—it's about presence. Mothers everywhere are turning their daily lives into platforms of influence, income, and impact. Whether you're building a business or becoming a thought leader, personal branding helps people trust, remember, and buy from you. This chapter helps you position yourself online with authenticity and clarity.

�� 1: Instagram and LinkedIn for Moms

Problem: Moms often underestimate their story or feel unqualified to build an online identity.

Insight: Instagram is where you connect emotionally. LinkedIn is where you build authority.

Solution:

- Instagram: Share daily life, wins, fails, and behind-the-scenes.
- LinkedIn: Share thought leadership, professional wins, and insights.

Practical Tip: Start with a clear bio, professional photo, and 3 content pillars (story, skill, offer).

Affirmation: My online presence is purposeful. I show up with courage and clarity.

�� 2: Storytelling Through Motherhood

Problem: Moms think their everyday life isn't inspiring enough.

Insight: Real life is what creates connection. Your story makes people say, "Me too."

Solution:

- Share your journey: from fear to freedom, chaos to clarity.
- Use story prompts: "I used to... Now I..." or "What I learned from this moment was..."

Practical Tip: Write 5 short stories from your motherhood journey that shaped your mindset or message.

Affirmation: My story is powerful. Every experience has value and voice.

❖❖ 3: Building Trust with Your Audience

Problem: People won't buy from you if they don't trust you.

Insight: Trust is built through consistency, transparency, and real conversation.

Solution:

- Engage in comments and DMs.
- Be honest about your journey—wins and struggles.
- Show your face, your process, and your personality.

Practical Tip: Go live once a week. Share one real lesson from the week.

Affirmation: I lead with truth. My brand is built on connection, not perfection.

❖❖ 4: Social Media Monetization

Problem: Moms grow a following but don't know how to earn from it.

Insight: Your audience wants solutions—if you serve, you can sell.

Solution:

- Choose a monetization path: affiliate links, digital products, brand partnerships, or coaching.
- Create one small offer that solves one small problem.

Practical Tip: Promote affiliate links for products you already love and use daily.

Affirmation: My voice creates value. My content earns trust—and income.

❖❖ 5: Visual Branding & Niche Marketing

Problem: Inconsistent visuals confuse your audience and dilute your message.

Insight: Visual consistency builds recognition, which builds brand equity.

Solution:

- Define your brand vibe: bold, soft, minimalist, or vibrant.
- Use 2 brand colors, 1–2 fonts, and a style for your visuals.
- Be clear about who you serve and how.

Practical Tip: Create 5 Canva templates you can reuse for posts and stories.

Affirmation: I am a brand. I speak to my people with beauty, clarity, and care.

Final Reflection:

You don't need 10K followers to be powerful. You need purpose, presence, and consistency. The mom next door has stories, value, and magic. It's time the world saw her shine. And yes—that mom is you.

Chapter 11: Legacy—Leaving More Than Just Money Main Focus: Creating generational impact

Your legacy isn't just what you leave behind—it's what you live every day. It's in the way you speak, serve, and show up for your family, your community, and your purpose. This chapter shifts your thinking from short-term success to long-term impact, helping you design a life that echoes far beyond your presence.

❖❖ 1: Defining Your Legacy

Problem: Most people focus on wealth but ignore the wisdom they could pass down.

Insight: Your values, stories, and lessons are your most priceless assets.

Solution:

- Write your legacy statement: What do I want to be remembered for?
- Clarify your top 3 core values (e.g., courage, compassion, creativity).

Practical Tip: Record a 5-minute video for your kids sharing your dreams, beliefs, and advice for the future.

Affirmation: I live my legacy now. My daily actions reflect my deeper purpose.

❖❖ 2: Teaching Values Through Action

Problem: Kids often hear instructions but remember what they observe.

Insight: Legacy is modeled, not just taught.

Solution:

- Show consistency between what you say and what you do.
- Involve your children in acts of kindness, forgiveness, and gratitude.

Practical Tip: Create a "Value of the Month" ritual where your family practices one value together.

Affirmation: My values are visible. I lead by example, not by explanation.

◆ ◆ 3: Generational Storytelling

Problem: Important family lessons and stories are often lost with time.

Insight: Sharing your journey helps build identity and resilience in future generations.

Solution:

- Share personal stories of failure, faith, and breakthroughs.
- Create a family legacy book or journal.

Practical Tip: Start a Sunday "Story Hour" where you share life lessons over dinner or bedtime.

Affirmation: My story matters. I pass on strength through storytelling.

◆ ◆ 4: Giving Back as a Family

Problem: Legacy is often limited to inheritance rather than impact.

Insight: Philanthropy teaches empathy, gratitude, and shared responsibility.

Solution:

- Involve your kids in choosing a cause or creating a giving plan.
- Volunteer as a family or start a small family fundraising challenge.

Practical Tip: Designate a monthly "Give Day" to contribute time, talent, or money as a unit.

Affirmation: We give with joy. Our family impact multiplies beyond money.

◆ ◆ 5: The Emotional Will

Problem: Legal wills share instructions, but not emotion.

Insight: An emotional will passes on beliefs, traditions, and healing.

Solution:

- Write letters to your kids or record voice notes sharing your hopes, stories, and blessings.
- Include affirmations and encouragement for their life journey.

Practical Tip: Store your emotional will in a legacy box or cloud folder for future sharing.

Affirmation: My love lives on. My words outlive my presence.

Final Reflection:

Your legacy starts today—with every word, decision, and act of courage. It's not just about what you build, but who you become while building it. Your life is a living message. Make sure it says what your heart intends. Let your children inherit more than assets—let them inherit your truth, your example, and your belief in what's possible.

Chapter 12: The Morning Power Hour—Starting Your Day Like a Millionaire Mom Main Focus: Morning routines that energize and empower

How you start your day shapes how you lead your life. A chaotic morning leads to a chaotic mindset. A centered morning builds unstoppable momentum. For mothers, the first hour of the day is sacred—it's the one hour you can reclaim for yourself before the demands of motherhood and work begin. This chapter offers a blueprint to build a simple yet powerful morning ritual that sets you up for clarity, confidence, and productivity.

❖❖ 1: Designing Your Power Hour (Mindset, Movement, Planning)

Problem: Many moms wake up reacting—to alarms, kids, and messages.

Insight: Intentional mornings create emotional regulation and grounded energy for the rest of the day.

Solution: Break your Power Hour into 3 parts:

- **10 mins mindset**: gratitude, breathwork, prayer, or journaling
- **20 minutes of movement**: yoga, walking, stretching, or dancing
- **30 mins planning**: review goals, block time, affirmations

Practical Tip: Start with just 15 minutes, then gradually expand. The habit matters more than the duration.

Affirmation: I begin my day with peace. I own my morning and master my mindset.

❖❖ 2: Habit Stacking for Consistency

Problem: New habits are hard to maintain with unpredictable routines.

Insight: Habit stacking—linking new behaviors to existing ones—makes consistency automatic.

Solution:

- Attach habits to anchors: "After brushing teeth, I write 3 gratitudes" or "Before coffee, I breathe for 2 minutes."

- Use time-based or location-based cues (e.g., when I sit at my desk, I visualize).

Practical Tip: Choose one anchor and one new 3-minute habit this week.

Affirmation: My habits support my vision. Small routines create massive shifts.

❖❖ 3: Gratitude Journaling & Visualization

Problem: The brain often defaults to problems first thing in the morning.

Insight: Gratitude and visualization reset your emotional baseline to calm and empowered.

Solution:

- Write 3 things you're grateful for.
- Visualize one goal as if it's already done (feel the joy, peace, or pride).

Practical Tip: Keep a journal on your nightstand. Begin before you even leave the bed.

Affirmation: I am grateful for now. I am excited for what's coming.

❖❖ 4: Morning Meditations & Affirmations

Problem: Anxiety often kicks in before the day even starts.

Insight: Meditation regulates the nervous system and affirmations rewire your inner dialogue.

Solution:

- Use guided meditations. (Insight Timer, YouTube)
- Repeat 3–5 affirmations that support your current goals and identity.

Practical Tip: Record your affirmations in your voice and play them while getting ready.

Affirmation: I choose peace over pressure. My words shape my reality.

❖❖ 5: Energy-Boosting Habits (Hydration, Light, Breathwork)

Problem: Physical sluggishness derails productivity.

Insight: Your energy is a product of how you treat your body in the first 30 minutes of waking.

Solution:

- Drink warm lemon water or herbal tea.

- Expose yourself to sunlight.
- Do 10 deep breaths or 2 minutes of movement.

Practical Tip: Use the 5-5-5 rule: 5 deep breaths, 5 sips of water, and 5 sun salutations.

Affirmation: I activate my energy with ease. My body responds to my care.

Final Reflection:

You deserve a morning that belongs to you—not just your to-do list. When you claim your first hour, you reclaim your identity, focus, and flow. You don't need more time—you need more intention. And it starts with how you rise.

Chapter 13: Creating Your Vision Map—Goal Setting with Heart & Hustle Main Focus: Turning dreams into tangible, actionable plans

You don't just need goals—you need a map. A vision without strategy is just a wish, but a plan with emotion and clarity becomes a force of nature. This chapter helps you turn scattered ideas into structured goals rooted in purpose. You'll learn how to align your ambition with your values so that every step forward feels inspired, not forced.

❖❖ 1: Creating a Vision Board

Problem: It's easy to lose direction without a visual reminder of where you're going.

Insight: The brain is drawn to images. A vision board triggers the subconscious daily and builds focus.

Solution:

- Collect images, words, and symbols that reflect your desired life.
- Include visuals for health, money, family, purpose, and joy.

Practical Tip: Create a digital vision board on Canva or Pinterest—or print one and hang it near your workspace.

Affirmation: My dreams are alive. I see my future clearly and walk toward it daily.

❖❖ 2: SMART Goals + Intuitive Goals

Problem: Traditional goal-setting can feel cold or too structured for moms juggling multiple roles.

Insight: Blending logic with intuition ensures your goals are aligned and achievable.

Solution:

- SMART Goals: Specific, Measurable, Achievable, Relevant, Time-bound
- Intuitive Goals: How do I want to feel? Who do I want to become?

Practical Tip: Set 3 SMART goals for the quarter and 3 intuitive goals for your soul.

Affirmation: My goals are clear and aligned. I chase what matters to me—not just what looks good.

◆◆ 3: Quarterly Goal Mapping

Problem: Long-term plans often fail without checkpoints.

Insight: A 90-day window gives you enough time to make progress without losing motivation.

Solution:

- Break yearly goals into quarterly themes.
- Focus on one major outcome per 90 days.

Practical Tip: Use a wall planner or digital tool to track weekly steps toward your quarterly goal.

Affirmation: I make progress in cycles. Each season brings clarity and achievement.

◆◆ 4: Weekly Reflections and Reviews

Problem: Without reflection, it's hard to know what's working.

Insight: Weekly reviews build self-trust, confidence, and sharper strategy.

Solution:

- Ask: What went well? What felt hard? What do I need to change?
- Celebrate every win—no matter how small.

Practical Tip: Set aside 20 minutes every Sunday for a goal check-in and emotional reset.

Affirmation: I reflect with honesty and move with purpose. My review fuels my evolution.

◆◆ 5: Accountability Systems for Busy Moms

Problem: It's easy to fall behind when no one's watching.

Insight: External or internal accountability systems help you follow through without burnout.

Solution:

- Join a mastermind, find a goal buddy, or create a reward system.

- Use habit trackers, alarms, or coaching apps.

Practical Tip: Choose one accountability system to implement this week. Track progress and reward consistency.

Affirmation: I am supported. I show up for my goals because they matter to me.

Final Reflection:

Your vision isn't too big—it's just waiting for structure. Map it. Speak it. Break it down. Chase it with heart and hustle. Because dreams don't come true through wishing—they come alive through aligned action, daily faith, and fierce clarity.

Chapter 14: Mom Boss Mindset—Rewiring Confidence Daily Main Focus: Cultivating deep self-belief and resilience

Confidence isn't something you're born with—it's something you build daily. As a mother, the world may doubt your potential, but your self-worth must never waver. The Mom Boss Mindset is about learning to trust your voice, act with courage, and reprogram your thoughts to serve—not sabotage—your goals. This chapter empowers you to install unshakable self-belief using science-backed and soul-centered tools.

❖❖ 1: Power Posing & Body Language

Problem: Confidence often disappears when we feel unseen, judged, or overwhelmed.

Insight: Studies show body posture impacts hormones and self-perception. Stand tall and your mind follows.

Solution:

- Practice power poses daily (arms up, shoulders back, chin lifted).
- Smile and take up space even when you don't feel confident yet.

Practical Tip: Strike a 2-minute power pose before a tough conversation, recording, or pitch.

Affirmation: I hold my space with pride. My body mirrors my inner strength.

❖❖ 2: Confidence Journaling

Problem: Self-doubt thrives in silence and unchallenged thoughts.

Insight: Writing reactivates the rational mind and grounds emotions.

Solution:

- Daily prompts: "Today, I'm proud of...," "A time I was brave...," "What success looks like for me..."
- Use journaling to create your own evidence of worth.

Practical Tip: Keep a "Confidence Log" where you collect compliments, wins, and brave actions.

Affirmation: I am proud of who I'm becoming. My confidence grows with my truth.

❖❖ 3: Affirmation Scripting

Problem: Negative thoughts loop when left unchecked.

Insight: The brain believes what it hears repeatedly—especially when spoken in your own voice.

Solution:

- Write 10 identity-based affirmations (e.g., "I am a magnetic leader," "I handle challenges with grace").
- Speak and record them. Listen daily.

Practical Tip: Script one "future truth" statement every week and visualize it as if it's already happening.

Affirmation: I speak life over my future. I am already her.

❖❖ 4: Visualization for Fearless Action

Problem: Fear holds back decision-making and bold steps.

Insight: Visualization rewires the nervous system and prepares the brain for new behaviors.

Solution:

- Visualize your day in advance: see yourself handling calls, creating, leading, and selling.
- Add emotion: feel the pride, ease, or joy of completing your tasks.

Practical Tip: Create a 3-minute "Morning Movie" where you mentally play your day's best-case scenario.

Affirmation: I act from belief, not fear. My future is familiar because I've seen it in my mind.

❖❖ 5: Confidence-Building Micro Wins

Problem: Big goals feel overwhelming and out of reach.

Insight: Small, intentional actions done consistently build identity and self-trust.

Solution:

- Set daily "micro wins" (posting content, emailing a client, saying no to something draining).
- Celebrate progress over perfection.

Practical Tip: Use a wall tracker or digital checklist to mark each day's win—even if it's just showing up.

Affirmation: I celebrate every step. My confidence compounds daily.

Final Reflection:

Confidence is not found—it's built. One small promise at a time. One bold move at a time. One "I did it anyway" moment at a time. Your power is not a someday destination—it's a muscle you strengthen every morning, every message, every step. You are not becoming confident. You already are. Now act like it.

Chapter 15: Time to Hire Help—Outsourcing Without Guilt Main Focus: Delegation for Freedom and Focus

You are powerful—but you are not meant to do it all. Superwoman is a myth. Sustainable success is built on support. Hiring help, whether at home or in business, doesn't make you less capable—it makes you more strategic. This chapter will help you redefine delegation, overcome guilt, and learn how to outsource with clarity and confidence.

❖❖ **1: How to Outsource Affordably**

Problem: Many moms think they can't afford help—or don't know where to start.

Insight: Help doesn't have to be expensive. Small, strategic support unlocks massive mental freedom.

Solution:

- Start with small tasks: grocery delivery, cleaning, childcare swaps, and part-time VAs.
- Use platforms like Fiverr, Upwork, UrbanClap, or local community groups.

Practical Tip: Budget 10% of your monthly business income for help. Reinvest in your energy.

Affirmation: Asking for help is powerful. I invest in ease and expansion.

❖❖ **2: Delegating Home Tasks (Cleaning, Meals, Childcare)**

Problem: Moms carry the invisible load of running the home, often in silence.

Insight: Delegating doesn't mean you're lazy—it means you're leading. Home is a shared responsibility.

Solution:

- Create a task chart for family members.
- Batch cook or use meal delivery once a week.

- Hire part-time help for cleaning or laundry.

Practical Tip: List your weekly tasks and star the ones only *you* can do. Outsource or automate the rest.

Affirmation: I release the burden of doing it all. My home flows because I lead with clarity.

❖❖ 3: Hiring VAs, Designers, and Editors for Your Business

Problem: Doing everything in your business slows growth and kills creativity.

Insight: Delegating low-impact tasks frees you to focus on high-value activities like sales and vision.

Solution:

- Hire a VA for admin, social media scheduling, or email.
- Hire a designer on Fiverr or Canva Pro for visuals.
- Use editors for eBooks, video, or content.

Practical Tip: Start with one task you hate doing and outsource it for 30 days.

Affirmation: I delegate with confidence. I build a business supported by brilliant people.

❖❖ 4: Overcoming Guilt and Control Issues

Problem: Moms often feel shame for needing help—or anxiety about "letting go."

Insight: Guilt is a byproduct of outdated expectations. Control comes from fear, not strategy.

Solution:

- Remind yourself: Support is a leadership skill, not a weakness.
- Practice releasing control in safe, low-stakes areas.

Practical Tip: Journal, "What am I afraid will happen if I delegate this?" Replace fear with facts.

Affirmation: I trust others. I release control and welcome flow.

❖❖ 5: Focusing on Your Zone of Genius

Problem: Being busy doesn't equal being productive.

Insight: Your greatest growth happens when you focus on what only *you* can do.

Solution:

- Define your Zone of Genius: What brings results and lights you up?
- Spend 70% of your time here. Delegate the rest.

Practical Tip: Time audit your week. How much time do you spend on your genius vs. your chores?

Affirmation: I am the visionary. My job is to lead, not to carry everything alone.

Final Reflection:

You weren't meant to wear every hat forever. Delegation is not a luxury—it's a legacy move. When you allow others to support your journey, you multiply your energy, time, and income. Let go to rise. Hire help. Lead well. Expand freely.

Chapter 16: The Power of Saying No—Protecting Your Energy Main Focus: Setting boundaries to honor your well-being

Saying "yes" to everything is often praised—but for mothers building a life of purpose, the real power lies in the "no." No to overcommitment. No to guilt-driven obligations. No to things that pull you away from your peace, goals, and joy. This chapter shows you how saying no is not rejection—it's redirection toward what truly matters.

❖ ❖ 1: Boundaries in Business and Parenting

Problem: Many moms feel drained because their days are ruled by everyone else's needs.

Insight: Boundaries protect your energy, priorities, and peace.

Solution:

- Define your "non-negotiables" in time, communication, and responsibilities.
- Practice enforcing limits kindly but firmly.

Practical Tip: Use scripts like "That doesn't work for me" or "Let me check and get back to you" before committing.

Affirmation: I protect my peace. My boundaries are a gift, not a wall.

❖ ❖ 2: Scripted Ways to Decline Politely

Problem: Saying "no" feels rude or uncomfortable.

Insight: A graceful "no" can actually strengthen relationships when done with respect.

Solution:

- "I'm honored you thought of me, but I'll need to pass."
- "Right now I'm focused on something else that requires my full attention."
- "I appreciate the invite, but I'm not available."

Practical Tip: Create your own go-to "no scripts" for social, business, and family requests.

Affirmation: I say no with love. My words honor my priorities.

◆◆ 3: Releasing People-Pleasing Tendencies

Problem: Moms often feel responsible for keeping everyone else happy.

Insight: People-pleasing is a coping mechanism, not a life strategy.

Solution:

- Reflect on what you fear losing by saying "no."
- Reframe: "When I say no to others, I say yes to myself."

Practical Tip: Journal on past situations where saying yes felt like self-abandonment. Rewrite the ending.

Affirmation: I am not here to please everyone. I am here to honor my path.

◆◆ 4: Identifying Your Energy Drains

Problem: Constant giving to the wrong people, tasks, or thoughts leaves you depleted.

Insight: Your energy is your most limited resource—treat it like a budget.

Solution:

- List your top 5 energy boosters and top 5 drains.
- Eliminate or limit energy leaks—whether people, apps, or habits.

Practical Tip: Do a weekly "energy audit" and schedule more of what replenishes you.

Affirmation: I protect what fuels me. I release what drains me.

◆◆ 5: Building a YES List Aligned With Your Goals

Problem: Without clarity on your goals, you end up saying yes to distractions.

Insight: A strong YES list makes it easier to confidently say NO.

Solution:

- Define your top 3 goals for the month.
- Align your schedule and commitments with these.

Practical Tip: Post your YES list somewhere visible—review before taking on new commitments.

Affirmation: I say YES to my growth. I choose what expands me.

Final Reflection:

Saying no is an act of self-respect. It is not your job to carry everything, fix everyone, or be everywhere. Every "no" makes space for your dreams, your peace, and your next level. This isn't about becoming cold—it's about becoming clear.

Chapter 17: Mompreneur Marketing 101—Visibility Without Burnout Main Focus: Simple, authentic strategies to grow your brand

Marketing doesn't have to feel like manipulation or overwhelm. When done with intention and soul, it becomes a bridge between your message and the people who need it. As a mompreneur, your time is precious—so this chapter is all about creating smart visibility systems that amplify your presence without sacrificing your peace.

◆ ◆ 1: Content Batching & Scheduling Tools

Problem: Posting daily drains energy and disrupts family flow.

Insight: Content batching saves hours and prevents burnout.

Solution:

- Dedicate 1–2 hours weekly to create content in bulk.
- Use scheduling tools like Buffer, Later, or Canva's Content Planner.

Practical Tip: Choose 3 themes (e.g., education, lifestyle, inspiration) and batch 3 posts for each weekly.

Affirmation: My content flows with ease. I show up consistently without chaos.

◆ ◆ 2: Repurposing One Idea into Many Formats

Problem: Moms think they need to create something new for every platform.

Insight: One idea can become five pieces of content with smart formatting.

Solution:

- Turn one blog post into a reel, a carousel, a podcast, an email, and a story.
- Focus on solving one problem from different angles.

Practical Tip: Use a Google Doc to store core messages and reuse them across platforms.

Affirmation: One idea. Multiple voices. Infinite impact.

❖❖ 3: Personal Storytelling in Brand Voice

Problem: Generic content doesn't connect.

Insight: People buy from people. Your story is your magnet.

Solution:

- Share wins, struggles, transformations, and day-in-the-life moments.
- Stay relatable, not rehearsed. Show the journey, not just the outcome.

Practical Tip: Use the "Hook – Heart – Help" format: Start with emotion, share truth, and give a takeaway.

Affirmation: My story sells with soul. My journey inspires action.

❖❖ 4: Free vs. Paid Promotions

Problem: Many moms don't know when or how to invest in ads.

Insight: Organic reach builds trust. Paid ads accelerate exposure.

Solution:

- Start with organic growth: hashtags, collaborations, live sessions, and email lists.
- Test paid promotions only when your offer is clear and proven.

Practical Tip: Run a ₹1000 Facebook ad trial targeting moms with your best post.

Affirmation: I market with wisdom. I invest with purpose.

❖❖ 5: Building a Content Calendar

Problem: Random posting creates inconsistency and confusion.

Insight: A content calendar aligns your message with your goals.

Solution:

- Plan one month in advance using themes, dates, and calls to action.
- Use Excel, Trello, or a printable calendar.

Practical Tip: Theme your days: Monday—Motivation, Wednesday—Wisdom, Friday—Family/Behind the Scenes

Affirmation: My content is organized and intentional. I show up with clarity.

Final Reflection:

Marketing is not shouting—it's serving. It's showing up consistently and generously with your truth. You don't need to be everywhere—you just need to be intentional where you are. When done with love and clarity, your message will find the hearts it's meant to reach. Visibility doesn't have to drain you. It can elevate you—and those watching you rise.

Chapter 27: From Hustle to Harmony—Redefining Success on Your Terms Main Focus: Letting go of "doing more" and choosing "being aligned"

The goal is not to do everything—it's to do what matters most. Build a success model based on your soul.

- Letting go of hustle culture
- Building a slow business with deep impact
- Rest as a business strategy
- Creating space to receive
- Inner alignment for outer results

Chapter 18: Time Is Your Currency—Managing It Like a CEO Mom

Main Focus: Time mastery strategies tailored for moms

Every mother knows the feeling of time slipping through her fingers. The minutes between lunch and naptime. The hours juggling work and bedtime routines. The late-night hours spent catching up on dreams. Time is the one resource you can't earn more of—but you can learn to manage it like a millionaire mom.

This chapter helps you shift from overwhelmed to organized. From scattered to strategic. From reactive to intentional. Because your time isn't just a schedule—it's a statement of what you value.

❖❖ 1: Time-Blocking for Mothers

Problem: Without structure, days blur into reactive chaos—leaving you drained and distracted.

Insight: Time-blocking gives visual clarity and focus. It creates room for creativity, rest, and ambition.

Solution: Divide your day into color-coded blocks: focused work, family time, self-care, admin, and free flow.

Practical Tip: Start with 3 blocks per day—morning (focus), afternoon (flexible), and evening (family).

Tool: Use Google Calendar, a printable planner, or time-blocking sticky notes.

Affirmation: I create space for what matters. My calendar honors my dreams.

❖❖ 2: Productivity Hacks for Home-Based Entrepreneurs

Problem: Working from home can blur boundaries between "work mode" and "mom mode."

Insight: Tiny productivity tweaks can reclaim hours without sacrificing presence.

Solution:

- Use the Pomodoro Technique (25 mins focus + 5 mins break).

- Work in themed days (Content Day, Admin Day, Client Day).
- Batch similar tasks (emails, videos, errands).

Practical Tip: Keep a whiteboard near your workspace with your 3 top daily priorities.

Affirmation: I work with purpose. Every moment is maximized with intention.

◆◆ 3: Family Calendar Management

Problem: Conflicting schedules create tension, miscommunication, and missed moments.

Insight: A family that plans together, thrives together. When everyone's needs are visible, harmony is possible.

Solution:

- Use a shared digital calendar (Google Calendar, Cozi app).
- Host "Sunday Syncs" with your family to review the week.
- Post a visible weekly planner on the fridge for everyone.

Practical Tip: Color-code each family member's tasks and responsibilities.

Affirmation: My home runs on harmony. Our calendar reflects unity and peace.

◆◆ 4: Prioritizing Tasks Around Kids' Schedules

Problem: Trying to force productivity into chaotic, child-led days leads to frustration.

Insight: Aligning tasks with your family rhythm enhances flow and reduces resistance.

Solution:

- Schedule high-focus work during nap times or early mornings.
- Use "light focus" periods for admin, emails, and brainstorming.
- Embrace flex time for creativity and play.

Practical Tip: Create a "Mom Mode Matrix"—label tasks as Deep Work, Light Work, and Family Work.

Affirmation: I align my energy with my family's rhythm. My life flows with grace and intention.

Chapter 19: Detox Your Digital Life—Reclaiming Focus in a Noisy World Main Focus: Managing screen time for clarity and peace

We live in the noisiest era in history—and it's stealing our peace. For moms juggling parenting, work, and purpose, constant digital distractions erode attention, creativity, and connection. This chapter helps you create healthier digital habits so your phone becomes a tool—not a trap—and your mind regains its spaciousness.

◆◆ 1: Phone-Free Mornings & Nights

Problem: Starting and ending your day with screens fuels anxiety and disconnection.

Insight: Bookending your day with intention instead of noise changes everything.

Solution:

- Set a no-phone window: 1 hour after waking, 1 hour before bed.
- Replace scrolling with rituals: reading, journaling, and breathwork.

Practical Tip: Leave your phone in another room with an analog alarm clock.

Affirmation: I begin and end my days in peace. My mind deserves rest.

◆◆ 2: Screen Limits for Moms and Kids

Problem: Excess screen time affects focus, emotions, and family bonding.

Insight: Healthy digital boundaries benefit the whole family.

Solution:

- Create device-free zones (e.g., dinner table, bedroom).
- Set tech-free time blocks with your kids (e.g., Sunday afternoons).

Practical Tip: Use screen time management apps or phone grayscale mode to reduce overstimulation.

Affirmation: I choose presence over pixels. My attention is sacred.

�� 3: Unsubscribing & Decluttering Inboxes

Problem: Email overload causes mental clutter and constant urgency.

Insight: Digital minimalism creates mental space for true priorities.

Solution:

- Unsubscribe from newsletters you don't read.
- Create folders for "Important," "Reply Later," and "Read for Growth."

Practical Tip: Block 30 minutes monthly for a digital declutter session.

Affirmation: I am organized and focused. My digital space reflects my clarity.

�� 4: Focus Apps and Website Blockers

Problem: Mindless scrolling breaks concentration and creates guilt.

Insight: Tools can help you create digital discipline and flow.

Solution:

- Use tools like Forest, Freedom, or Cold Turkey to block distracting apps/sites.
- Schedule deep work blocks where only essential apps are enabled.

Practical Tip: Try a 25/5 productivity cycle—25 minutes of work, 5 minutes of stretching/breathing.

Affirmation: I control my focus. I use technology with purpose.

�� 5: Creating a Digital-Free Zone at Home

Problem: Technology often invades every corner of family life.

Insight: Your physical space influences your inner state. You need screen-free sanctuaries.

Solution:

- Choose a room or corner in your home where no devices are allowed.
- Fill it with books, cushions, candles, plants—whatever soothes you.

Practical Tip: Use this space daily for family time, meditation, or solo reflection.

Affirmation: I create space for stillness. My home nourishes my mind and spirit.

Final Reflection:

A clear mind begins with a clear screen. You don't need to disappear from the digital world—you just need to lead it, not let it lead you. Reclaim your focus. Reclaim your peace. Reclaim the quiet where your creativity and clarity can finally breathe.

Chapter 20: Detox Your Digital Life—Reclaiming Focus in a Noisy World Main Focus: Managing screen time for clarity and peace

We live in the noisiest era in history—and it's stealing our peace. For moms juggling parenting, work, and purpose, constant digital distractions erode attention, creativity, and connection. This chapter helps you create healthier digital habits so your phone becomes a tool—not a trap—and your mind regains its spaciousness.

❖ ❖ 1: Phone-Free Mornings & Nights

Problem: Starting and ending your day with screens fuels anxiety and disconnection.

Insight: Bookending your day with intention instead of noise changes everything.

Solution:

- Set a no-phone window: 1 hour after waking, 1 hour before bed.
- Replace scrolling with rituals: reading, journaling, and breathwork.

Practical Tip: Leave your phone in another room with an analog alarm clock.

Affirmation: I begin and end my days in peace. My mind deserves rest.

❖ ❖ 2: Screen Limits for Moms and Kids

Problem: Excess screen time affects focus, emotions, and family bonding.

Insight: Healthy digital boundaries benefit the whole family.

Solution:

- Create device-free zones (e.g., dinner table, bedroom).
- Set tech-free time blocks with your kids (e.g., Sunday afternoons).

Practical Tip: Use screen time management apps or phone grayscale mode to reduce overstimulation.

Affirmation: I choose presence over pixels. My attention is sacred.

◆◆ 3: Unsubscribing & Decluttering Inboxes

Problem: Email overload causes mental clutter and constant urgency.

Insight: Digital minimalism creates mental space for true priorities.

Solution:

- Unsubscribe from newsletters you don't read.
- Create folders for "Important," "Reply Later," and "Read for Growth."

Practical Tip: Block 30 minutes monthly for a digital declutter session.

Affirmation: I am organized and focused. My digital space reflects my clarity.

◆◆ 4: Focus Apps and Website Blockers

Problem: Mindless scrolling breaks concentration and creates guilt.

Insight: Tools can help you create digital discipline and flow.

Solution:

- Use tools like Forest, Freedom, or Cold Turkey to block distracting apps/ sites.
- Schedule deep work blocks where only essential apps are enabled.

Practical Tip: Try a 25/5 productivity cycle—25 minutes of work, 5 minutes of stretching/breathing.

Affirmation: I control my focus. I use technology with purpose.

◆◆ 5: Creating a Digital-Free Zone at Home

Problem: Technology often invades every corner of family life.

Insight: Your physical space influences your inner state. You need screen-free sanctuaries.

Solution:

- Choose a room or corner in your home where no devices are allowed.
- Fill it with books, cushions, candles, plants—whatever soothes you.

Practical Tip: Use this space daily for family time, meditation, or solo reflection.

Affirmation: I create space for stillness. My home nourishes my mind and spirit.

Final Reflection:

A clear mind begins with a clear screen. You don't need to disappear from the digital world—you just need to lead it, not let it lead you. Reclaim your focus. Reclaim your peace. Reclaim the quiet where your creativity and clarity can finally breathe.

Chapter 21: How to Handle Haters—Staying Grounded in a Loud World Main Focus: Resilience in the face of criticism and online noise

The more you grow, the more visible you become. And with visibility often comes criticism—some fair, some baseless. For moms pursuing big dreams, learning how to stand tall in the face of negativity is a skill, not just a trait. This chapter equips you to protect your peace, maintain focus, and grow your confidence—no matter the noise.

❖❖ 1: Understanding the Psychology of Trolls

Problem: Online haters trigger self-doubt and emotional overwhelm.

Insight: Hate is often projection. It says more about them than it does about you.

Solution:

- Recognize the difference between feedback and trolling.
- Don't argue with what doesn't deserve your energy.

Practical Tip: Respond only when feedback is respectful and constructive. Otherwise—delete, block, move on.

Affirmation: I protect my energy. Not all criticism deserves my response.

❖❖ 2: Strengthening Your Inner Voice

Problem: External opinions can overpower your internal truth.

Insight: Your inner voice is your compass. Strengthening it gives you immunity to noise.

Solution:

- Daily affirmations and mirror work
- Journal your wins and truths so you have evidence of your power.

Practical Tip: Write a "confidence script" to read on hard days.

Affirmation: My truth is louder than their opinions.

❖❖ 3: Strategies for Handling Negativity Online

Problem: Negativity can spiral into fear, shame, or over-explaining.

Insight: Your platform is your space. You set the tone.

Solution:

- Set clear community guidelines.
- Use comment filters and block features freely.
- Maintain your boundaries unapologetically.

Practical Tip: Prepare 3 go-to responses for negative comments. Or decide to not engage at all.

Affirmation: I choose peace over performance. I lead with presence, not people-pleasing.

❖❖ 4: When to Respond and When to Block

Problem: Confusion around what's worth your time and what's not.

Insight: Not everything needs a defense. Silence is a powerful boundary.

Solution:

- Respond when it opens growth or learning.
- Block when it's toxic, unproductive, or draining.

Practical Tip: Ask, "Is this about growth or ego?" If ego—let it go.

Affirmation: My peace is my filter. I engage with wisdom, not emotion.

❖❖ 5: Anchoring Back to Your Purpose

Problem: Haters distract you from your mission.

Insight: Your why is your shield. Anchoring to your purpose dissolves doubt.

Solution:

- Revisit your mission, vision, and audience.
- Create a "Why Wall" with quotes, notes, and affirmations from your community.

Practical Tip: Keep screenshots of testimonials, thank-you messages, and progress milestones.

Affirmation: I rise for those I serve. My work speaks louder than their words.

Final Reflection:

You weren't meant to be liked by everyone. You were meant to lead the ones who need your light. Stand tall. Speak true. Let criticism sharpen you—not shatter you. Because the woman who can rise through noise becomes the woman who changes the world.

Chapter 22: Celebrate Yourself—Anchoring Confidence Through Milestones Main Focus: Building momentum through self-recognition

Too often, moms move from one task to the next without acknowledging their wins. Celebration is not just joy—it's fuel. It reinforces your identity as a capable, worthy woman. This chapter helps you create meaningful rituals to honor your growth.

- The psychology of positive reinforcement
- Weekly, monthly, and milestone celebrations
- Creating personal reward systems
- Journaling progress and micro wins
- Sharing success without shame

Chapter 24: The Power of Female Friendships—Sisterhood and Support Main Focus: Building a circle that uplifts and energizes

A million-dollar mom doesn't rise alone. This chapter is about nurturing powerful relationships with other women.

- Identifying your circle of influence
- Navigating jealousy and comparison
- Mastermind groups and accountability partners
- Saying goodbye to draining friendships
- Hosting empowering circles at home or online

Chapter 25: Selling With Soul—Authentic Marketing That Converts Main Focus: Offering your gifts with confidence and clarity

Chapter 26: Selling With Soul—Authentic Marketing That Converts
Main Focus: Offering your gifts with confidence and clarity
Selling is a service. This chapter teaches soulful, mom-friendly sales strategies.

- Overcoming fear of selling
- Creating magnetic offers
- Conversational selling vs. pushy tactics
- Sales scripts with heart
- Follow up with love, not pressure.

Parenting While Pursuing Purpose—Embracing the Dual Role
Main Focus: Integrating your ambitions with your parenting journey
Core Message: You're not choosing between being a great mom and a great visionary. You're becoming both—powerfully.

There's a myth society loves to sell women: that you must choose. Choose between nurturing your children and nurturing your dreams. Choose between feeding your baby and feeding your ambition. Choose between being present at home and being present in your own story.

But here's the truth bomb, and it's one every million-dollar mother must know: **you can do both, and you can do both with power, grace, and purpose.**

We live in a time where the role of a mother is evolving. Today's woman isn't confined to the home or the boardroom—she can thrive in both. But embracing this dual role doesn't mean it comes without challenges. It means you get to redefine the script. It means you get to *design* a life where purpose and parenting coexist, not compete.

❖❖ 1: Mompreneur Guilt Detox

Guilt is the silent killer of dreams for too many mothers. You feel guilty when you're working and not with your children. And then you feel guilty when you're with your children and not working on your goals. It's a lose-lose—until you break the cycle.

Solution: Reframe guilt as *evidence of your passion*. You care deeply—that's a strength, not a weakness. Set emotional boundaries by defining your working hours, honouring your priorities, and **detoxing guilt** through honest conversations with your kids. They don't need a perfect mom. They need a present, passionate one.

❖❖ 2: Aligning Your Values with How You Parent and Work

You don't have to lead two lives—your values at home and your values at work can be the same. If you believe in empathy, discipline, creativity, and resilience—those values should reflect in both your parenting and your projects.

Exercise: Create a "Values Vision Board" where you list 5 core values. Ask yourself how each one shows up at home and in your entrepreneurial or career life. This keeps your energy aligned and reduces burnout caused by inner conflict.

❖❖ 3: Letting Kids See the "Real" You

Children don't need the edited, filtered version of you. Let them see the struggle and the courage it takes to chase your purpose. Let them see you fail, try again, and come back stronger.

Practical Tip: Involve your kids where possible—let them help pack orders, watch you brainstorm, or be a part of small victories. Say, "Mom is nervous about this presentation, but I'm going to give it my best." You're not hiding stress—you're teaching resilience.

❖❖ 4: Creating Structure That Supports Both Roles

Chaos is the enemy of progress. While flexibility is essential, **structure is liberating**. Design a weekly rhythm that honors both your children's needs and your purpose-driven priorities.

Tool: Use time blocks. Example:

- 6:30–8:30 AM: Family time
- 9 AM–1 PM: Deep work
- 2–4 PM: Client calls
- 5–7 PM: Playtime or dinner
- 8–9 PM: Wind-down + light creative tasks

Include buffers. Life with kids is full of surprises—but structure helps you stay centered.

❖❖ 5: When to Ask for Grace and When to Go All In

There will be weeks when the dream takes a backseat—and others when dinner is ordered three nights in a row. That's okay. Know when to **ask for grace**, forgive yourself, and regroup. Equally, recognize the moments when it's time to **go all in**—to push, to show up, to build.

Mindset Shift: You're not behind. You're not failing. You're a mother building an empire—brick by brick, hug by hug, meeting by meeting.

❖❖ Final Reflection:

Being a mother is not a pause button on your life's purpose—it's a magnifier. Your children are not obstacles to your dreams. They're the reason you dream bigger, work harder, and rise stronger.

So the next time you feel torn between being a great mom or a visionary—**remember that you are both. Fully. Fiercely. Unapologetically.**

Chapter 26: The Entrepreneurial Motherhood Map—Balancing Growth and Grace Main Focus: Navigating entrepreneurship with harmony, not hustle

Main Focus: Offering your gifts with confidence and clarity

Selling is a service. This chapter teaches soulful, mom-friendly sales strategies.

- Overcoming fear of selling
- Creating magnetic offers
- Conversational selling vs. pushy tactics
- Sales scripts with heart
- Follow up with love, not pressure.

Parenting While Pursuing Purpose—Embracing the Dual Role

Main Focus: Integrating your ambitions with your parenting journey

Core Message: You're not choosing between being a great mom and a great visionary. You're becoming both—powerfully.

There's a myth society loves to sell women: that you must choose. Choose between nurturing your children and nurturing your dreams. Choose between feeding your baby and feeding your ambition. Choose between being present at home and being present in your own story.

But here's the truth bomb, and it's one every million-dollar mother must know: **you can do both, and you can do both with power, grace, and purpose.**

We live in a time where the role of a mother is evolving. Today's woman isn't confined to the home or the boardroom—she can thrive in both. But embracing this dual role doesn't mean it comes without challenges. It means you get to redefine the script. It means you get to *design* a life where purpose and parenting coexist, not compete.

❖ ❖ 1: Mompreneur Guilt Detox

Guilt is the silent killer of dreams for too many mothers. You feel guilty when you're working and not with your children. And then you feel guilty when you're with your children and not working on your goals. It's a lose-lose—until you break the cycle.

Solution: Reframe guilt as *evidence of your passion.* You care deeply—that's a strength, not a weakness. Set emotional boundaries by defining your working hours, honouring your priorities, and **detoxing guilt** through honest conversations with your kids. They don't need a perfect mom. They need a present, passionate one.

◆◆ 2: Aligning Your Values with How You Parent and Work

You don't have to lead two lives—your values at home and your values at work can be the same. If you believe in empathy, discipline, creativity, and resilience—those values should reflect in both your parenting and your projects.

Exercise: Create a "Values Vision Board" where you list 5 core values. Ask yourself how each one shows up at home and in your entrepreneurial or career life. This keeps your energy aligned and reduces burnout caused by inner conflict.

◆◆ 3: Letting Kids See the "Real" You

Children don't need the edited, filtered version of you. Let them see the struggle and the courage it takes to chase your purpose. Let them see you fail, try again, and come back stronger.

Practical Tip: Involve your kids where possible—let them help pack orders, watch you brainstorm, or be a part of small victories. Say, "Mom is nervous about this presentation, but I'm going to give it my best." You're not hiding stress—you're teaching resilience.

◆◆ 4: Creating Structure That Supports Both Roles

Chaos is the enemy of progress. While flexibility is essential, **structure is liberating.** Design a weekly rhythm that honors both your children's needs and your purpose-driven priorities.

Tool: Use time blocks. Example:

- 6:30–8:30 AM: Family time
- 9 AM–1 PM: Deep work
- 2–4 PM: Client calls
- 5–7 PM: Playtime or dinner
- 8–9 PM: Wind-down + light creative tasks

Include buffers. Life with kids is full of surprises—but structure helps you stay centered.

❖❖ 5: When to Ask for Grace and When to Go All In

There will be weeks when the dream takes a backseat—and others when dinner is ordered three nights in a row. That's okay. Know when to **ask for grace**, forgive yourself, and regroup. Equally, recognize the moments when it's time to **go all in**—to push, to show up, to build.

Mindset Shift: You're not behind. You're not failing. You're a mother building an empire—brick by brick, hug by hug, meeting by meeting.

❖❖ Final Reflection:

Being a mother is not a pause button on your life's purpose—it's a magnifier. Your children are not obstacles to your dreams. They're the reason you dream bigger, work harder, and rise stronger.

So the next time you feel torn between being a great mom or a visionary—**remember that you are both. Fully. Fiercely. Unapologetically.**

Chapter 27: Parenting While Pursuing Purpose—Embracing the Dual Role Main Focus: Integrating your ambitions with your parenting journey

The goal is not to do everything—it's to do what matters most. Build a success model based on your soul.

- Letting go of hustle culture
- Building a slow business with profound impact
- Rest as a business strategy
- Creating space to receive
- Inner alignment for outer results

? Letting Go of Hustle Culture

The Myth of More

We've been taught that success requires sacrifice, sleepless nights, and endless hustle. But actual achievement doesn't come from constant grind—it comes from clarity, boundaries, and aligned action.

Redefining Productivity

Productivity isn't about doing everything—it's about doing the right things purposefully. Shift your focus from being busy to being intentional.

Breaking the Addiction to Overwhelm

If your self-worth is tied to your exhaustion, it's time to rewrite the narrative. You are worthy even in rest, stillness, and simplicity.

Choosing Peace Over Pressure

Success with peace of mind is not only possible—it's powerful. Let go of the pressure to prove and rise from a place of purpose instead.

? Building a Slow Business with Deep Impact

The Power of Patience

Fast wins fade. But a business built with depth and care lasts. Choose sustainability over speed. Build a brand, not just a buzz.

Intentional Growth

A slow business is not a small one—it's a smart one. You grow when you're ready, not rushed. Expand from a place of vision, not urgency.

Energy-Respectful Strategy

Slow business respects your energy cycles. You build when you're in flow, pause when needed, and never compromise your well-being for quick wins.

Purpose Over Performance

Your work isn't just a profit machine—it's a mission. A slow business focuses on changing lives, not just checking boxes.

? Rest as a Business Strategy

Permission to Pause

Rest is not laziness. It's an act of self-respect and long-term planning. When you rest, you reclaim your strength and creativity.

Recharging Your Mental Power

Your brain needs breaks. Strategic rest boosts problem-solving, emotional regulation, and decision-making—key skills for any entrepreneur.

Modelling Self-Care for Others

When you honour rest, you lead by example. Your team, family, and community will learn that burnout isn't a badge of honor.

Scheduling Rest Intentionally

Build rest into your weekly calendar—like meetings. Digital detoxes, quiet time, and mini-breaks are as essential as any strategy session.

? Creating Space to Receive

Healing the "Over-Giver" Pattern

Many women give endlessly, but struggle to receive. It's time to believe that you are worthy of being supported, celebrated, and paid well.

Abundance is a Cycle

You give. You receive. You circulate. The more space you make—mentally, physically, emotionally—the more aligned abundance flows in.

Receive Without Guilt

Whether it's a compliment, a client, or a care package, practice receiving with gratitude, not guilt. Receiving is not selfish—it's sacred.

Practical Tip: Create Receiving Rituals

Start a gratitude journal. Open yourself to compliments. Say "yes" when help is offered. Let the universe meet you halfway.

? Inner Alignment for Outer Results

The Power of Alignment

When your thoughts, actions, and values align—you stop forcing and start flowing. Alignment is the shortcut to fulfillment.

Clarity Creates Confidence

Knowing who you are and what you stand for brings unwavering confidence. You stop second-guessing and start acting with authority.

Making Aligned Decisions

Choose work that excites your soul. Say yes only to what matches your purpose. Say no without guilt when it doesn't.

Daily Check-In Practice

Ask yourself: "Is this in alignment with my vision?" Let that guide your time, energy, and opportunities.

Chapter 28: Healing the Inner Child—Becoming the Woman You Needed Main Focus: Emotional healing and self-acceptance

Every mother carries an inner child. Through deep self-reflection and healing, you can unlock your full power.

- Identifying childhood wounds that block growth
- Reparenting rituals and forgiveness
- Visualisation for healing
- Journaling conversations with your younger self
- Turning pain into purpose

? Healing the Inner Child – Becoming the Woman You Needed

1. Identifying Childhood Wounds That Block Growth

Every powerful woman was once a little girl who may have been misunderstood, unseen, or made to feel "too much" or "not enough." These early emotional wounds often go unnoticed, but they quietly write the script of our adult lives.

Do you find yourself afraid of rejection? Struggling to trust? Believing you're unworthy of rest, success, or love unless you "earn" it?

These are not flaws. They are echoes—traces of childhood moments when your needs weren't met, your emotions weren't honoured, or your brilliance was dimmed to fit in. Identifying these wounds is not about blaming others. It's about understanding yourself.

Start with reflection:

What patterns keep repeating in your life?

What triggers you most in relationships, business, or motherhood?

When did you first start feeling "not enough"?

Awareness is the first and most radical step toward healing. When you recognize the origin, you stop reacting to pain and start responding with power.

2. Reparenting Rituals and Forgiveness

Once you've seen your wounds, it's time to do something revolutionary: become the mother you always needed.

Reparenting is the daily practice of nurturing your inner child with love, boundaries, care, and compassion. It's speaking to yourself, not with criticism, but with tenderness. It's saying:

"You're safe now."

"I'm proud of you."

"You don't have to be perfect to be loved."

Forgiveness is part of this journey. Forgiving doesn't mean forgetting the pain—it means freeing yourself from it. You forgive so that you can move forward unchained.

Create daily reparenting rituals:

A gentle morning affirmation like, "Little me, I've got you today."

Lighting a candle in honour of the girl you once were.

Touching your heart and repeating, "You're not alone anymore."

Remember: every time you care for yourself with love, you heal not just you—but the generations before and after you.

3. Visualization for Healing

The mind doesn't know the difference between real and vividly imagined. That's why visualization is such a powerful healing tool. When you picture your younger self and give her what she never received, you actually begin to rewrite your emotional blueprint.

Sit quietly. Breathe deeply. Picture yourself at 5... 7... 12. What is she wearing? What is she afraid of? What does she long for?

Now visualize yourself walking up to her. Hug her. Smile at her. Say things she needed to hear:

"You are not a burden."

"Your voice matters."

"You're allowed to be joyful."

Watch her eyes light up. Feel the healing ripple back through your soul. This isn't make-believe. It's medicine.

Make this a weekly practice. It reprograms your subconscious and builds emotional safety from the inside out.

4. Journaling Conversations With Your Younger Self

Your inner child has a voice. Journaling gives her a page to speak.

Begin with the prompt: "Dear Little Me..." and let your pen move. Let her cry, shout, whisper, laugh. Ask her questions:

"What do you wish I knew?"

"What did you need back then?"

"What are you still scared of today?"

Then respond as your current self. Let her know she's no longer alone. She has a protector now—you.

This sacred dialogue builds trust between your past and present selves. It bridges the gap between who you were and who you are becoming.

Even just 5–10 minutes of writing a day can become a lifeline of emotional integration and healing.

5. Turning Pain Into Purpose

The final and most transformative step is alchemy: turning pain into purpose.

Every heartbreak you've endured, every tear you've cried, every night you questioned your worth—has prepared you for the work you're meant to do. Nothing was wasted. Your journey, your scars, your survival—they carry wisdom the world desperately needs.

Whether you:

Write a book

Start a business

Mentor someone else

Raise emotionally whole children

You are not defined by what broke you. You are defined by how you rebuilt.

Your inner child didn't go through all that just for you to survive. She went through it so you could thrive—and lead others home to themselves too.

You are no longer a product of pain. You are the embodiment of purpose.

? Final Reflection:

You don't need to become someone else to be whole. You just need to become someone your younger self would feel safe with, proud of, and loved by.

She's still inside you—waiting, watching, wondering if you'll come back for her.

This is your moment to say:

"I see you. I hear you. I love you. And together, we rise."

Chapter 29: Becoming Her—Embodying the Future You Now Main Focus: Stepping into the identity of your higher self

It's not just about doing more—it's about becoming more. Be guided to act, think, speak, and create like the woman you are becoming.

- Visualisation practices
- Embodiment rituals
- Dressing, speaking, and choosing as your future self
- Emotional alignment with identity
- Manifestation meets micro action.

Your journey doesn't end at a milestone. It transforms. These final chapters invite you to live the million-dollar mindset—not someday, but every single day.

? Becoming Her: Embodying the Future You Now

You don't become your highest self by waiting for the "right time." You become her by living today as if she already exists—because she does. She's within you, waiting to be claimed.

1. Visualization Practices – See It, Feel It, Become It

Visualization is not wishful thinking—it's neural rewiring. The brain doesn't know the difference between imagined success and lived success. When you visualize your next-level life with emotion and detail, your mind begins creating a roadmap to make it real.

Morning Practice: Close your eyes and see your ideal day. Where do you wake up? What do you wear? What does your bank account say? Who are you helping?

Feel the Frequency: It's not enough to "see" it—you must feel the gratitude, peace, joy, and confidence of that future self.

Create a Vision Vault: Keep a vision board on your phone or mirror. Revisit it daily. Let it remind you of what's coming.

? If you see it daily, your reality will rise to meet it.

2. Embodiment Rituals – Shift from Thinking to Living

Embodiment means moving, thinking, and choosing from the energy of your future self. It's about becoming the woman you dream of—before the dream arrives.

Morning Ritual: Light a candle, sip tea with intention, move your body with joy. Create a sacred moment that connects you to her energy.

Walk like Her: How would she enter a room? How would she hold herself at a meeting? Practice posture, presence, and poise.

Speak like Her: Would she apologize unnecessarily? Would she shrink to fit in? Or would she speak truth, grace, and conviction?

? You don't wait to feel like her—you practice being her until it feels natural.

3. Dressing, Speaking & Choosing as Your Future Self

You send signals to your subconscious with everything you wear, say, and choose. Every micro-decision is a vote for the woman you are becoming.

Dress with Intention: You don't need designer labels. You need pieces that make you feel radiant, powerful, feminine, or focused—whatever reflects HER.

Speak in Future Tense: Replace "I hope" with "I am." Replace "someday" with "today." Own your identity before the evidence appears.

Decide with Confidence: Your future self doesn't beg for permission. She sets standards, honors time, and says no when needed. Start acting from her wisdom today.

? Every outfit, every word, every yes or no—it all builds your next chapter.

4. Emotional Alignment with Identity – Tune In, Don't Chase

If you want to become her, you have to feel like her first. Success isn't just strategy—it's state of being. Align your emotions with your goals to bring them into reality faster and more peacefully.

Check Your Frequency: Ask yourself daily: "Am I acting from fear or faith? Stress or success? Doubt or confidence?"

Name the Feeling: Your future self likely feels grounded, grateful, powerful, peaceful. Practice bringing those feelings into your NOW—even before the outer results.

Daily Emotional Calibration: Breathe. Journal. Affirm. Move. Realign yourself whenever you feel off-course.

? Your emotions are your GPS. When they match your vision, the destination finds you faster.

5. Manifestation Meets Micro Action – Dream Bold, Move Small

Manifestation without action is fantasy. Action without alignment is burnout. You need both. Think big—but move daily, with intention.

Start Small but Strategic: One pitch. One post. One brave email. One walk-in-your-worth decision. You don't have to leap—you just have to begin.

Track Your Wins: Micro-wins build momentum. Create a tracker or journal that records each day's bold action—no matter how small.

Reverse Engineer Your Vision: Want a six-figure business? Start by showing up on Instagram today. Want a book deal? Write 500 words today. Don't wait. Create.

? Every micro action is a spark. Keep striking the match until the fire catches.

? Final Reflection

You are not chasing your future self. You are activating her.

She doesn't need more time. She needs your belief.
She doesn't need a perfect plan. She needs your presence.
She doesn't live "someday"—she's ready now.

So breathe. Straighten your shoulders. Say her affirmations. Wear her colors. Walk in her pace. Think with her clarity.

Because when you decide to become her now, your world has no choice but to reflect that truth.

Chapter 30: Creating a Home That Supports Your Dreams Main Focus: Designing your environment for peace and productivity

Your home should inspire, not exhaust you. This chapter teaches space alignment for emotional and creative flow.

- Decluttering for clarity
- Designating a creative corner
- Feng Shui and energy flow basics
- Minimizing chaos in family zones
- Making your home feel like your sanctuary

? Creating a Home That Supports Your Dreams
(Designing Your Environment for Peace, Power & Productivity)

Your home isn't just a shelter—it's an energy ecosystem. It either fuels your vision or silently drains it. For a mother building her empire, her space must reflect the peace, purpose, and power she wants to embody. Let your home become your sanctuary—and your strategy.

1. Decluttering for Clarity – Clear Space, Clear Mind

Clutter isn't just physical—it's emotional weight. A messy environment creates mental fog, emotional fatigue, and decision overwhelm. Every item in your space either supports or suffocates your focus.

Start small: One drawer, one shelf, one corner at a time.

Ask: "Does this item support who I'm becoming?"

Let go with gratitude: Bless the item for its service and release it if it no longer aligns.

? Decluttering is self-respect in action. When you clear space in your environment, you create space in your soul.

2. Designating a Creative Corner – Claim Your Sacred Space

You need a space that belongs to YOU—not shared with toys, bills, or endless laundry.

Pick a corner: A desk, a window nook, or even a small table where your dreams live.

Keep tools of creation nearby: Your journal, laptop, books, affirmations, mood board.

Make it sacred: Add candles, flowers, crystals, quotes—anything that lifts your energy.

? This isn't just a corner—it's a commitment. A physical symbol of your inner work, your voice, your vision.

3. Feng Shui & Energy Flow Basics – Move Energy with Intention

Feng Shui isn't about superstition—it's about energetic alignment. When your home flows, your life flows.

Front Door: Keep it clean and welcoming. It's where opportunities enter.

Workspace: Face a wall or open space—not a cluttered hallway or a mirror.

Bed Placement: Keep your headboard against a solid wall to symbolize support.

Add plants for vitality, use mirrors to expand light, and ensure pathways are clear. Energy should circulate like breath—easy, open, alive.

? When energy flows freely in your home, your creativity, abundance, and peace will too.

4. Minimizing Chaos in Family Zones – Structure for Harmony

Family areas—like kitchens, living rooms, and play areas—can easily become zones of chaos. But with a few shifts, they can promote connection and calm.

Rotate toys/books weekly: Keeps things fresh without constant clutter.

Create "zones": A reading corner, a play mat, a no-device dinner table.

Involve your kids: Let them co-design systems. When they help organize, they help maintain.

? Home doesn't have to be perfect—it needs to feel functional, loving, and peaceful for the season you're in.

5. Making Home Feel Like Your Sanctuary – Healing Begins Where You Live

You deserve to walk into a space that exhales with you.

Use calming colors: Soft whites, earthy tones, or whatever soothes your nervous system.

Create sensory moments: Diffuse essential oils, play soft music, dim the lights after 8 PM.

Display reminders of joy: Photos, travel souvenirs, handwritten goals, affirmations.

Your home should be your soft landing, your reset button, your inner temple. When the world feels too loud, let your space whisper peace back into your spirit.

? A woman who feels safe and inspired in her home becomes unstoppable outside it.

? Final Reflection

Your home doesn't have to look like a magazine. It has to feel like you.

Not the you from yesterday. Not the chaotic "trying-to-keep-up" you.

But the future you. The Million Dollar Mother who wakes up with clarity, moves with purpose, creates with passion—and rests with joy.

Design your space to hold your dreams. Because where you live, you lead.

Steps To Step Fully Into Your Power As A Million-dollar Mother

❖ ❖ **Steps to Step Fully into Your Power as a Million-Dollar Mother**

1. Define Your Version of "Having It All."

What to do: Redefine success in your terms.

- What does a fulfilled day look like for *you*?
- Is it about impact, peace, freedom, love, or contribution?
- Let go of Pinterest-perfect expectations.
- Say, "My success looks like balance, joy, and authenticity."

Your empire should fit your soul, not society's scoreboard.

2. Celebrate Your Dual Identity—Creator & Caregiver

What to do: Embrace both roles as part of your power.

- Stop apologising for being ambitious.
- Stop minimising the work of mothering.
- Understand that the same love that builds a child can build a company.
- Say aloud, "I can desire both hugs and high returns."

You are not torn—you are *woven*.

3. Create a Rhythm, Not a Race

What to do: Lead your life with pace, not pressure.

- Prioritise what matters most weekly, not daily hustle traps.
- Build in rest, reflection, and real joy.
- Use seasons: creation, launch, rest, and recalibration.
- Your journey is not a sprint—it's a sustainable masterpiece.

4. Speak Life into Yourself Daily

What to do: Power your day with affirmations and compassion.

- "I am building a life of freedom and love."
- "I am the safe space and the spark."
- "I rise, even when tired. I shine, even when unseen."

Speak to yourself like you would to your daughter—**with fierce encouragement.**

5. Build with Purpose, Not Just Pressure

What to do: Let your business, career, and goals reflect your inner truth.

- Choose clients, products, or services aligned with your values.
- Say "no" to what drains—even if it pays.
- Create not just for revenue, but for **resonance**.
- Let every move be part of your message.

The million-dollar mother's empire is not measured in zeros—it's measured in **impact, energy, and legacy**.

◆◆ **Final Takeaway**

You are no longer just surviving motherhood. You are **sculpting a dynasty**—one loving action, one bold decision, and one aligned step at a time.

This is your time.

This is your story.

And you, dear queen, are the **Million-Dollar Mother.**

Keep rising. Keep leading. Keep loving.

◆◆ **Final Words: You Are the Legacy**

Dear Reader,

If you've made it this far, it's because you know one thing deep in your bones—**you were never meant to live small.**

You are not just a mother. You are a visionary. A dream-keeper. A cycle-breaker. A leader in heels, slippers, or barefoot in the kitchen.

You've balanced breakdowns with breakthroughs. Quiet moments with bold moves. Chaos with calm.

And through it all—you've never stopped becoming.

This book was never just about money. It was about **worth**. It was never only about building businesses. It was about **building belief**.

And it was never simply about raising children. It was about **raising a new world** through the powerful, purposeful life of one extraordinary woman—you.

You, who dared to rewrite the rules.

You, who learned to lead with love.

You, who became the mother, the mogul, and the miracle—all at once.

As you turn the final page, remember this:

Your story matters.

Your mission is sacred.

And your motherhood is not the end of your ambition—it's the most beautiful part of it.

So go ahead. **Build the empire. Hug your babies. Sign the deals. Say the affirmations. Take the naps. Heal the wounds. Break the patterns.**

Do it all—in your own way, in your own time, with your own fire.

You are a million-dollar mother.

And this world has been waiting for everything you're becoming.

With love, belief, and deep respect,

– Amulya Mishra

A Personal Request from the Author

Dear Reader,

Thank you for taking this journey with me through *Million-Dollar Mother*.

If this book inspired you, uplifted you, or helped you reclaim your strength—I would be truly honored if you would take **just 1–2 minutes** to leave a review.

Your words—no matter how brief—can help other women discover this book, feel seen, and step into their own power.

Whether you're a working mom, a stay-at-home dreamer, or a woman building something beautiful while raising a family—**Your voice matters..**

❷ ❷ Leave a review on Amazon or wherever you purchased this book. Your feedback helps me write better, serve more, and grow this empowering community of Million-Dollar Mothers.

From one dreamer to another,

Thank you for reading.

Thank you for believing.

Thank you for becoming.

With gratitude,

– Amulya Mishra